Hank Aaron

BILL GUTMAN

Revised and updated from AT BAT

GROSSET & DUNLAP
Publishers   New York

For Beth

Copyright © 1974 by Bill Gutman
All Rights Reserved
ISBN: 0-448-05739-5

A Tempo Double Book
Tempo Books is registered in the U.S. Patent Office

Published simultaneously in Canada
Printed in the United States of America

ACKNOWLEDGMENTS

The author wishes to thank the following people for their help in supplying background material for this book: Bob Hope of the Atlanta Braves, as well as the publicity department of the team; and Kevin Fitzgerald at *Sport* Magazine.

Hank Aaron

Henry Aaron

HENRY AARON HAS got to be one of the most remarkable athletes of the twentieth century. Now statements like that aren't tossed around like frisbees on a Southern California beach. Yet few people would dare to disagree, especially if they've followed Hammerin' Hank's exploits of the last few seasons, as outfielder for the Atlanta Braves.

For at the end of the 1973 baseball season Hank Aaron was just one home run away from tying the immortal Babe Ruth's career record of 714 four baggers. And as the 1974 season opened, the whole country was watching and waiting for the magic moment.

But his homerun record is just one of the reasons why Henry Aaron is a remarkable athlete. It may be his most dramatic and important achievement, but it is by no means his only one. He has already broken or is approaching a host of all-time marks, many of them falling to his consistency and durability, matched by a rare few throughout the entire history of the sport.

In fact, Hank does it with an easy, relaxed style that has almost served to mask his talents until a few short years ago. Until he started piling up a list of impressive numbers, Bad Henry just hadn't received the recognition accorded some of the other stars of the era. He was always a quiet, private man, and you might say his style of play was the same.

He lacks the on-field flare of a Willie Mays and the off-field outspokenness of a Roberto Clemente. He doesn't have the bulging muscles of a Mickey Mantle or the uniquely distinctive batting stance of a Stan Musial. He's conservative in both his dress and his lifestyle. For these reasons it has taken years for most people to be really aware of Henry Aaron. One writer put it this way:

"Media people swirling around Henry are dismayed to find him basically colorless, free of apparent neurosis—a man who in a different circumstance would be dismissed as downright normal."

Even black baseball fans have been slow to adopt Hank as one of their own.

"Not all the brothers are plugged into Hank Aaron because he's not electrifying," said black journalist Frank McRae. "He doesn't reflect what has come to be the image of the 'soul man.' In the minds of many blacks, Hank is not black enough."

Despite some truth in what Mr. McRae has said, Hank is proud of himself and his people, and he's given his time and energy to black causes with increasing frequency during the past few years. Perhaps the reason he did not become more involved sooner was his total and complete dedication to the game of baseball. For within Henry Aaron burns a fire, a fire that drives him to peak performance year after year. And he's said that the lack of recognition for this has bothered him for a long time.

"I always used to read the names Mickey Mantle and Willie Mays first. Then Hank Aaron. Well, I've worked pretty darned hard to get my name up front."

The pride that drives the man makes itself felt in many ways. You've got to know the entire Hank Aaron story to truly appreciate the greatness of his skills. He's turned 40-years-old as the new season begins and for him the end is clearly in sight. But when it comes, the entire sports world will applaud the accomplishments of number 44.

Just when did all the excitement over Henry Aaron begin? When did the slim slugger begin to lose his anonymity and begin attracting the attention he so long deserved. Well, it wasn't really so long ago. Let's set the scene.

On the night of June 10, 1972, the Atlanta Braves were in Philadelphia for a game against the hometown Phillies. It was a cool evening, the heat and humidity of summer not yet arrived. Players sat close together in the dugouts, most of them wrapped in warm-

3

up jackets to keep out the dampness and chill that was in the air.

It was still early in the season, but it was already obvious that neither team was going anywhere fast. The Phils, in fact, had one of the worst teams in baseball. The Braves, on the other hand, had a power-laden lineup, but little pitching to back it up. They lacked the needed balance to make a serious run at the pennant.

Consequently, there wasn't much of a crowd on hand that night, but it didn't deter the Brave hitters. They went to work and pounded the pill all over the lot. By the sixth inning, Atlanta had a big lead and the Phils had their umpteenth pitcher, a righthander named Wayne Twitchell, in the ballgame.

Once again the Braves opened up, quickly loading the bases. Out of the Atlanta dugout ambled number 44, Henry Aaron. The veteran slugger looked almost unconcerned, detached, as he made his way slowly to the plate, gazing out at Twitchell while he walked.

In the box he settled into his familiar stance, midway right side, left foot slightly closer to the plate. He held his bat high, right elbow extended upward. He was loose and relaxed.

Twitchell took a deep breath. The young pitcher didn't want to get burned any more. He decided he had the strength to blow the ball past Aaron. He wound and delivered. Ball one! Aaron didn't budge. Twitchell threw again. This was a strike, inside cor-

4

ner. Aaron rested the bat on his shoulder until the pitcher was ready. Then it came up again.

For the third time Twitchell threw his fastball. This time Aaron wanted it. He took a short stride, then snapped the bat around, his powerful wrists giving it a sharp whip. Seconds later it was Twitchell who was whipping around, watching the flight of the ball out into left centerfield. It was too late for him to do anything but watch it pass over the fence for a grand slam home run.

Hank Aaron trotted slowly around the bases. He saw the three runners scoring ahead of him, smiled slightly, then came across the plate to grab the congratulating hands that awaited him. Twitchell scuffed at the mound angrily. He had just become an unwilling part of baseball history.

The home run was the 38-year-old Aaron's tenth of the season. But more important, it was the 649th of his long career, and it enabled him to pass 41-year-old Willie Mays and move into sole possession of second place on the all-time list. In addition, it was the 14th grandslammer of his career, and that tied a National League record previously held by the late Gil Hodges.

Why was the home run so significant? Simply because it brought into crystal clear focus an undeniable fact of baseball life. Hammerin' Hank Aaron had an excellent chance of breaking one of the game's most revered records, Babe Ruth's career mark of 714 home runs.

It was a record many thought would stand forever. Even when Roger Maris broke Ruth's single-season mark of 60, by belting 61 in 1961, baseball traditionalists pointed to the enlarged schedule as a reason for Maris' success, and added, "Nobody will ever touch the Babe's career mark."

Many believed that to be true. Then in the middle 1960s, two sluggers—Mickey Mantle and Willie Mays—climbed over the 500 mark. A few years later they were joined by Aaron, and some people began to talk about the trio in terms of their ultimate capabilities.

But Mantle was forced to the sideline by injuries and retired with 536 round trippers to his credit. Mays marched on, driving over the 600 mark, and for the first time there was a legitimate challenger for the Ruthian standard. It was Willie's race against time.

Then, in 1971, people realized it wasn't Willie's race alone. Aaron, too, whacked number 600, and he was chasing Mays. Some three years younger and in seemingly better health than Willie, Hank continued to belt the ball. He slammed 47 homers, a career high, as a 37-year-old in 1971. And when the season ended, he had 639, trailing Mays by just nine home runs.

When Aaron hit his homer off Twitchell that night in Philadelphia, he served notice that he was the only one with a chance. Mays was near the end of the line. He wasn't playing regularly and hadn't hit a single home run in the first two months of the season.

Suddenly all the talk centered around Aaron. Writers and broadcasters began looking at the books. They found that the homer mark wasn't the only one within Aaron's range. The great rightfielder of the Braves was near the top of the all-time list in games played, at-bats, runs scored, hits, total bases, runs batted in and extra base hits.

None of this should have come as a surprise to so many people, but it did. The reason is simple. Henry Aaron is a quiet superstar. He plays the game with skills matched only by a select few. He does his job, day after day, without creating any kind of furor, without verve or flash. Furthermore, he played his entire career in Milwaukee, then Atlanta, never having had the benefit of the big-city press, such as is the case in New York, or on the west coast. As a consequence, Aaron's skills and achievements went largely unnoticed for a great number of years.

"I know I'm not flashy," Hank Aaron once said. "But I don't try to be. I just play my natural way. It's almost the same as the way I dress. I have good clothes and dress well, but not flashy. That's just my way and I can't change it."

His easy style of play affected others the same way. Billy Bruton, who was the Braves' centerfielder when Hank came up in 1954, once said, "I used to say a prayer every time Hank went after a fly ball. It always looked as if he'd never get there. But after he was around awhile and I saw the things he could do, I never worried about him again."

And another former teammate, Felipe Alou, who

7

played both with and against Aaron, said this: "I never realized how good Henry was until I played alongside him every day. In the outfield he gives everyone so much of the right field line, yet he gets to every ball hit out there in an easy way."

If Aaron's teammates didn't see his greatness at first, how were the fans and writers supposed to see it? It was a long time before Hank's talents were fully appreciated by the vast majority of baseball people. And by then he was creeping up on a host of all-time records.

Now there is only admiration and respect for this great slugger, a lifetime .300 hitter, fine outfielder and simply marvelous all-around ballplayer. He deserves to be ranked right up there with the best of them and he will be.

Still looking trim at six feet, 180 pounds, Henry Aaron doesn't appear to be a man of 40 years. Only his face is fuller, otherwise he looks much like the shy, 20-year old youngster who reported to the Braves as a rookie in 1954. And he's proud of the fact that he's been so durable, his only serious injury having been a broken ankle in September of that very first year.

"I take good care of myself," Hank says. "I know I'll only go as far as my body takes me. I always come into spring training at 188 pounds or so and I'm down around 180 when the season begins."

You can't refute the Aaron logic. The results speak for themselves. In 1972, Henry put 34 more home runs to his total of 639. Add that up. The answer is 673. And the difference between 673 and 714 is 41. Barring injury or a sudden decline in his skills, most people feel that Hank Aaron will be baseball's new all-time home run champion sometime during the 1974 season.

As is his style, Henry is not acting overly excited about it. With each passing day, month, year, he's been asked more and more about his chances of setting a new mark. He always answers coolly and rationally.

"Sure, I think about it (the record)," he says. "I think I can do it if I stay healthy and if I have a strong man batting behind me. That way, they can't pitch around me."

Then Hank talked about another phenomenon that's come his way. "I get a lot of letters asking me not to break the record. They're not vicious letters, mind you, but apparently there is so much tradition and sentiment involved with Ruth's record that people don't want to see it broken.

"I guess a lot of people will be disappointed if anyone tops Ruth. But if I do it, I'll fully expect someone else to come along and top me some day."

Henry Aaron has been a realist ever since he came to the majors. But when he was a boy, he had a lot of the dreamer in him, and he needed that quality to get where he is today.

Hank was born in Mobile, Alabama, on February 5, 1934, the third child of Herbert and Estella Aaron.

9

Four other children were to follow, so the Aaron family was a large one.

The Aarons came to Mobile just two years before Henry was born. Before that, they lived in Camden, Alabama, a small farm town near Mobile. Both Mr. and Mrs. Aaron knew what it was like to work all day in the fields and they wanted to improve the lot of their growing family.

So they moved to the Down-the-Bay section of Mobile, where many other poor black families lived. Mr. Aaron was a very hard-working man. He soon got a job as a boilermaker's assistant and made enough money to move his family to a better neighborhood, the Toulminville section of Mobile. That's where young Henry grew up.

As a youngster, Henry was shy and withdrawn. He didn't like playing with the other boys and often stayed very close to home. Even when he was five years old, he had no desire to explore the world. He just liked staying around his mother and playing in the safety of his back yard.

"Henry could spend hours by himself when he was a boy," Mrs. Aaron said. "He used to go out in the yard and play with a top for hours on end, just spinning and watching it. But I'll never forget one day when I walked out there. He was playing with the top as usual, only this time he wasn't spinning it, he was hitting it with a baseball bat."

That was the first indication of Hank's attraction to the game. It was just a few years later, when he was eight, that the youngster saw major league baseball for the first time.

In those days, baseball teams trained in Florida during the spring, then made their way north by train, stopping every day or so to play a game in the cities along the route. That way, the players had additional practice time, and many more people had a chance to get a glimpse of the major league game.

Mobile was a regular stop along the way, and Henry would go out and sit by himself in the bleachers at Hartwell Field, watching some of the great players in action. He saw Musial, Williams, Feller and DiMaggio—and followed their exploits with wonderment. DiMaggio had a special fascination for him. He liked the Yankee Clipper's style and grace, and when he'd come home he'd always announce:

"I'm gonna play ball like Jo DiMaggio when I grow up."

Still, Henry played little ball with the other boys, preferring to throw a ball around with his older brother, Herbert, Jr., or with his Uncle Bubba. But he slowly got over his shyness and started playing more with the other boys. He really loved the game right from the start.

The United States was in the midst of World War II at that time, and for the next three years not many of the top stars came to Mobile. They were all in the service. By the time they returned in 1946, Henry had become an avid fan and good young ballplayer.

"I really can't say where I got my ability from,"

Hank explained. "My Daddy always worked very hard from the time I knew him, but I heard he was a good ballplayer when he was younger and I guess that's where I got some of it from.

"One thing I know about my father was that he hated laziness. I remember one time it was my turn to chop wood for the fire. I just didn't feel like doing it, so I chopped a small amount, then tried to pile it up so it looked like more. My Daddy didn't go for that. I got a good whipping for that one and learned not to be lazy when Herbert Aaron was around."

The year was 1946 when most of the top baseball stars returned from the war and started playing at Hartwell Field again. And this time Henry had a special reason for going, even if it meant skipping school. The Brooklyn Dodgers had a new player named Jackie Robinson and he was the first black man ever to play with a major league team.

Robinson's presence helped turn the dream into reality. Young Henry watched Jackie's progress during the next several years. He saw other young blacks joining major league teams. Now there was a chance that he could really play like Joe DiMaggio or Jackie Robinson. From that point on he thought of little else.

School really didn't mean much to him. And whenever there was a baseball game around, he skipped. One time, he was sitting in a local poolroom, listening to the Dodgers playing on the radio. Who should walk by? None other than Herbert Aaron. He brought his son home and the two had a long talk.

Hank told his father that he wanted to be a ballplayer. It was the only thing he was interested in.

"You can still be a ballplayer and have your education, too," Mr. Aaron said. He and his wife believed in education for all their children. But Henry had the answer.

"I can't learn much about playing ball in a classroom, can I?" he said.

"Listen," said Mr. Aaron. "I give you fifty cents to take to school with you every day for your lunch and whatever else you need. I take a quarter with me to work. That's because it's worth more to me to see you get an education than it is for me to eat."

It was obvious that Mr. Aaron was thinking of his youngster's welfare and Henry promised to finish high school. But he knew what he wanted and was determined to reach his goal.

By that time, Henry was playing a lot of softball around Mobile, and he was quickly gaining a reputation as the best young hitter around. The odd thing was that he batted crosshanded, with his left hand above his right on the bat. Even so, his wrists were already strong enough for him to whack line drives all over the field.

When he went to Central High, an all-black school in Mobile, he was an instant star. "Henry was the king-pin for two years," says his coach, Edwin Foster. "He was here for two years, and we lost only three games in that time. He was really a great player with us."

Hank was an infielder in those days, playing both second and short. He also played guard on the Central High football team for one year, but gave it up because he didn't want to risk an injury that would hamper his baseball career. Then, before his senior year, his parents decided to send him to the Josephine Allen Institute, a private school in Mobile where they thought he'd have a better chance to get ready for college.

When he was about fifteen and just starting to play at Central, the Dodgers held a tryout camp in Mobile. Henry rushed out with great expectations, but quickly learned a lesson in the law of survival. Every time he made a move to go out on the field or get a turn in the batting cage, a bigger boy pushed him out of the way. He never did get a chance to show his stuff and went home in tears. He realized then that he'd have to be more aggressive if he wanted to be a real ballplayer.

That's how he played the game from then on. One day shortly afterward, he was playing in a sandlot game when a man named Ed Scott approached him. Scott beckoned for Hank to come over after the game.

"How would you like to make some money, Aaron?"

Henry was puzzled. He wondered what Scott had in mind, but when the man added, "Playing baseball," Henry was all ears.

Ed Scott wanted Hank to play for the Mobile Black Bears, one of the best semi-pro teams in the area. The Bears met many of the top Negro League teams that passed through Mobile, and young Hank was excited at the opportunity to play with and against good ball-players, men much older than himself.

It took some convincing for Mrs. Aaron to go along with the idea, but she finally consented. Henry played for the Bears some evenings and on Sundays, operating at short and second, and hitting better than anyone.

The Bears' payroll came from the old-fashioned pass-the-hat system, with the fans contributing whatever they could. Players generally got from three to five dollars a game, depending on how well they played. Hank Aaron set records then also. Sometimes he did so well that they gave him ten dollars a game.

For two years, Henry played outstanding ball for the Bears. The older players liked and respected him. Late in the summer of 1951, the Bears scheduled a game with the Indianapolis Clowns, widely regarded as one of the best of the barnstorming Negro League teams in the country.

With many black ballplayers now beginning to filter into the major leagues. Negro League teams were feeling a talent squeeze and were on the lookout for fresh young ballplayers. And Henry Aaron was the bestlooking kid they'd seen in a long time.

Against the Clowns that August afternoon, Hammerin' Hank slammed a double and two singles, as well as making a couple of sparkling plays in the field. When the game was over, Bunny Downs, the Clowns' road manager, came looking for Hank.

Downs tossed a bevy of questions at the youngster, asking his age, whether he was still in school, when he graduated, what other positions he played.

To the last question, Henry said, "I'll play any position you want."

"That's what I like to hear," Downs replied. "Henry, how would you like to play baseball for the Indianapolis Clowns?"

Henry was stunned, and he recalls his reaction to this day. "I couldn't believe what the man was saying. But I didn't let him see how excited I was. I just sort of played it real casual and said something like, 'I don't see why not.' So he started telling me that he'd send me a contract as soon as I got out of high school and I could expect to hear from him. One reason I didn't show my excitement was that I didn't know if he was on the level. I figured I'd just wait and see."

Sure enough, right before he graduated from Josephine Allen Institute in June of 1951, Hank received a contract in the mail offering him $200 a month to play baseball for the Clowns.

The only problem was his parents. Mr. and Mrs. Aaron didn't know too much about baseball and didn't really understand what it meant to play professionally. They certainly couldn't imagine their son playing alongside established major league stars. For them, college was the best answer for Henry. He'd had a few scholarship offers, in fact, and they were determined for him to continue his education.

It took some mighty fancy talking for Henry Aaron

to convince his parents to let him play for the Clowns. But they saw how serious their son was about baseball and they didn't want to hold him back. So, in May of 1952, Henry got ready to leave home for the first time.

"I was really worried about Henry leaving home," said Mrs. Aaron. "He had never been away before and he hadn't even been around other people much. Now, all of a sudden, he was going out on his own with all these other people. I wasn't sure if he could handle it.

"All I could think of was a little boy, playing by himself in the back yard, or sitting in the house reading comics. I knew he was going to be homesick and I wished he was just a little older. But I knew he had to go. I gave him two dollars, packed up two pairs of pants, and made him two sandwiches. That was all he left home with."

So it was on the train and up to Winston Salem, North Carolina, where the Clowns were training for the upcoming season. Henry joined a team that had some disgruntled, older players. Some were bitter because the color line had been broken in the majors long after they were in their prime, their opportunity to play in the big leagues lost forever. Others were just worried about losing their jobs.

As a consequence, they didn't take to young, talented Hank Aaron with much friendliness. Few talked to him. He had trouble getting the proper equipment. He was alone and not enjoying his first experience in baseball at all.

"Henry was calling us up all the time," said Mrs.

17

Aaron. "He was homesick, just like I knew he'd be. He told us about how the older players were treating him. They were giving him a plain old hard time. He said he didn't even have a warmup jacket. He was alone there and thought maybe he should come home.

"I didn't know what to tell him. In one way, I wanted to tell him to come home, but I knew that wasn't right. He had worked so hard to get there. So I put his brother, Herbert, Jr., on the phone. Herbert was six years older than Henry and I knew Henry would listen to him.

"Herbert told Henry to stay. He reminded him of how badly he wanted to play baseball and that he shouldn't give up his big chance without a fight. Henry agreed, and said he'd stay with the Clowns."

Henry Aaron fought back the best way he knew. He became Hammerin' Hank and began tattooing the baseball. Before long, he was the team's leading hitter and run producer. Now the older players had to respect him.

There was one problem. Amazingly enough, Hank still hit crosshanded. It has to rank as one of baseball's great feats, that this youngster, batting incorrectly, holding the bat in an awkward fashion that prevented him from using all his power, was able to hit so well. Finally, one day, Syd Pollock, the owner of the Clowns, approached him.

"Henry, you're the team's best hitter," he told the

youngster. "But there's no way you'll ever make the majors batting that way. You've got to change."

Never one to ignore good advice, Hank began practicing with the correct grip, and pretty soon he found himself hitting the ball even harder, hanging liners all over the field, and smashing long, towering home runs. But it was a hard habit for him to break. He often found himself reverting to the crosshanded grip with two strikes on him and he had to make a conscious effort not to do it.

But when he finally broke the habit, he hit better than ever. The word about him was spreading. He wasn't with the Clowns three months when he was told that several big league scouts were already making inquiries about him. He reacted to the news with his usual detached air, but inside he was wild with excitement.

The Giants were the first team that expressed a real interest in Hank. But Syd Pollock wrote a letter to the Boston Braves, informing them about the young slugger. The Braves dispatched scout Dewey Griggs to take a look. The Clowns were due in Buffalo, New York, to play a doubleheader against the Kansas City Monarchs. Griggs was there.

To put it mildly, Hank Aaron was hot that day. He came to the plate nine times and banged out seven hits, including two long home runs. In the field, he started five double plays. Grigg's eyes almost popped out of his head.

In order for a major league team to get Henry's services, they had to buy his contract from Syd Pollock. Before long, both the Giants and Braves began to talk with Henry and with Pollock.

The Giants started it. They offered Henry a $300-a-month contract and said they'd send him right to a Class A minor league team. He'd be just a step from the majors and the offer was intriguing to him. But Dewey Griggs scoffed when he heard it.

"They're pikers," he said. "The Braves will pay you $350 a month and we'll start you off with a Class C team. That way, there won't be any pressure on you and you can work your way up at your own pace."

Henry was advised to go with the Braves. They made a little better offer and would send him to an easier club. He'd played with black teams all his life and there would be an amount of adjusting to be done.

When the Braves offered Syd Pollock $10,000 for Henry's contract, the deal was closed. Looking back at the turn of events that made Hank Aaron a Brave, a sportswriter said:

"It's too bad for the Giants that they didn't make a better offer. Could you imagine Hank Aaron and Willie Mays playing on the same team down through the years? What a combination! The whole face of baseball might have been different. With those two in the same lineup, the New York fans couldn't have stayed away from the Polo Grounds. Who knows, the Giants might never have left New York."

It's an interesting possibility, but it never came to

pass. Hank signed and was instructed to report to the Braves' Class C team at Eau Claire, Wisconsin. He said goodbye to the rest of the Clowns, got a handshake and a cardboard suitcase from Syd Pollock, and left. In return for the suitcase, Pollock had a $10,000 check from the Braves. So he didn't do badly for having had Aaron just a few short months.

As for Henry, he was another step closer to his dream. It seemed like only yesterday that he had been pleading with his parents for a chance to play with the Clowns, hoping it would lead him to the majors someday. Now, at the age of 18, he was already with the Boston Braves organization. It was all happening so fast.

But dazzled as he was by all that had occurred, he didn't let it affect his performance. At Eau Claire, he was an immediate sensation, his free-swinging style exciting the fans and driving in the runs.

Hank played in 87 games for Eau Claire during the last half of the 1952 season. He batted a solid .336, hit nine homers and had 61 runs batted in. In addition, he stole 25 bases and played a fine game at second base. He was named to the Northern League all-star team and was voted the league's Rookie of the Year. Henry Aaron was on his way.

"That Northern League pitching was really tough," he says now, looking back. "It was by far the toughest brand of ball I'd played up to then. But I was getting older and beginning to have more confidence in my ability than I ever had before."

Henry's greatest season was rewarded. At first, he was told that he'd be headed for the Milwaukee Brewers, the Braves' Triple A farm club. But before the season started, the Braves franchise was moved from Boston to Milwaukee, and the minor league Brewers were shifted to Toledo. At the same time, it was decided that Henry should play for Jacksonville, a Class A team in the South Atlantic or Sally League.

But Henry would have more than baseball to think about during the 1953 season. He and two other blacks were told that they would be breaking the Sally League color line that year. League cities were all located in the so-called deep south and there might be some problems. It didn't really turn out that way. There were a few tense moments, but no real trouble.

Blacks stayed in separate quarters, usually private homes in the Negro sections of town. Ironically, it worked out well, because, as Henry said, the people in the private homes always wanted to do everything to please them. They were proud to be helping ballplayers who might soon be in the major leagues. So Henry and his two teammates had home-cooked meals and comfortable beds. It was usually better quarters than the hotel where the white players stayed.

As for breaking the color line, Hank Aaron had his own approach.

"There was only one way to break the color line," he said, "and that was to play well. If you played good exciting baseball, most of the people don't remember what color you are."

Hank practiced what he preached. As soon as he stepped into a Jacksonville uniform he started hitting. Insults came out of the stands in one big southern city, but Hank and the others learned to ignore them, no matter how much it hurt. If anything, the slurs prodded Hank to hit even better.

Ben Geraghty was Hank's manager that year and the two grew very close. Geraghty liked and admired the youngster from Mobile and he knew that he had a future star in the making.

"Henry was the most relaxed kid I've ever seen," Geraghty said. "Nothing bothered him. During the long bus rides he'd always fall asleep. He could sleep anywhere.

"And he had a deadpan look about him so I never knew when he was pulling my leg and when he was serious. I remember one time in midseason I decided to change all the signs. Henry came up the next day and I gave him the new take sign. Well, he promptly hit a homer.

"When he got back to the dugout and I asked him why he didn't take the pitch, he told me that I gave him the hit sign. I said no, that was the old hit sign, but the new *take* sign. He just looked at me with that deadpan of his and said, 'Damn, I only got around to learning the signs yesterday.' I settled the issue the easy way. For the rest of the season I just let him hit away."

Henry hit away, all right, to the tune of 208 hits in just 137 games. He belted 22 homers, drove in 125 runs and led the league in hitting with a .362 average. He also topped the Sally League in hits, RBI's, doubles and runs scored. It came as no surprise when he was named the loop's Most Valuable Player by a wide margin.

Something else happened to Hank that year. He met a girl, Barbara Lucas, who was a business student at Florida A & M University. They began dating, fell in love and were married on October 6, 1953. Two days later, the Aarons were off on an unexpected honeymoon. The news came from Ben Geraghty.

"The Braves want to take a long look at your next spring," the jaunty manager said.

Henry felt his heart jump with excitement. Then Geraghty continued:

"They feel you'll have a better chance to make the club as an outfielder. You still have too much to learn about the infield and they feel they're pretty well set there. What they want is for you to play winter ball in Puerto Rico, as an outfielder. What do you say?"

Henry looked at Geraghty with his usual deadpan. "It's fine with me, as long as I don't have to speak Spanish."

Despite his reservations about the language barrier, Henry didn't mind going at all. It was perfect, an extended honeymoon for him and Barbara, plus playing baseball. And best of all, the next spring he'd have his first real chance at making a major league team.

Playing the outfield came easy to him. He wasn't worried at all about his fielding, and as for his hitting, that was as natural as eating a piece of pie. He was officially assigned to the triple A team at Toledo for the 1954 season, but he'd be training with the big club at Bradenton, Florida.

The 1954 Milwaukee Braves were considered a coming team in the National League. They already had some fine performers like pitchers Warren Spahn and Lew Burdette, catcher Del Crandall, outfielder Billy Bruton, infielders John Logan, Eddie Mathews and Joe Adcock. Most of them were still young ballplayers approaching their best playing years.

Two unsettled positions were leftfield and second base. Manager Charlie Grimm and general manager John Quinn engineered two trades that hopefully solved the problem. They acquired second baseman Daniel O'Connell from Pittsburgh and outfielder Bobby Thomson from the Giants. Thomson was the hero of the 1951 pennant with his dramatic playoff homer against the Dodgers. When he joined the club, Hank Aaron was sure he'd be spending the summer in Toledo.

Early in the spring, Henry didn't play much. He pinch hit, or pitch ran, not much more. The Braves wanted to work Thomson into their ballclub and he was getting most of the playing time. Young Aaron wasn't really getting a chance to show his stuff.

Then on March 15, fate took a hand. The Braves were playing an exhibition game against the Yankees. Henry made his customary pinch-hitting appearance, had already showered, and was standing under the bleachers drinking a coke and watching the remainder of the ballgame.

Thomson was up and promptly smacked a hard shot down the leftfield line. He dug around first and went sliding into second with a double. Then Henry noticed that Bobby wasn't getting up. He was twisting in pain on the ground. Minutes later he was being carried from the field on a stretcher, his ankle broken.

The next question was, who would take Thomson's place? Everyone tried to guess, but few people even mentioned Hank Aaron. Most of the newspaper people still didn't know him. But the day after Thomson's injury, manager Grimm walked slowly toward Henry in the clubhouse. Suddenly, he picked up the youngster's glove and tossed it to him.

"Here, kid," the old manager said. "You're my new leftfielder. The job's yours until someone takes it away from you."

Twenty-year-old Hank Aaron stood there openmouthed. It was the last thing he expected to happen. He figured veteran Jim Pendleton would get the first shot and he'd be on his way back to the minors. But he wasn't complaining. Then, before the start of the regular season, general manager Quinn made it official. He told Henry that the Braves had purchased his contract from Toledo.

"I was so happy to be in the big leagues that I just signed the contract Mr. Quinn put in front of me," Henry said. "I didn't even know what my salary was.

26

But I trusted Mr. Quinn and figured he'd take care of all the details."

Hank went hitless in his first major league game against Cincinnati. He was nervous and excited. He knew it would take him awhile to get used to the majors. But he felt better when he learned how much confidence manager Grimm had in him.

"Henry's not the spectacular type," Grimm told reporters. "He makes everything look easy out there. So we're not going to try to make another Willie Mays out of him. But mark my words, he'll be around long after Willie's gone."

The encouragement must have helped. On April 23, Hank blasted his first big league homer off veteran Vic Raschi of St. Louis. Two days later he whacked another, this time off crafty Stu Miller. Now he was sure he could hit major league pitching, and hit it with power.

From that point on, Hank was an everyday player, continuing to hit well and patrolling the outfield more than adequately. What's more, the Braves were in a pennant race, battling the Dodgers and Giants for the flag, so the youngster from Mobile was playing the game under pennant pressure and producing in the clutch.

On September 5, the Braves were just five games from the top and still considered to have a chance at winning it all. The team was in Cincinnati for a doubleheader. In the first game, Grimm decided to rest

27

his rookie and started the recovered Bobby Thomson in left.

Thomson got a hit in the seventh inning and Henry went in to run for him. Later in the game, Aaron batted on his own and doubled. He started the second game and stroked hits his first three times up. Then he came up again late in the game.

Henry felt good that day, relaxed and loose. He felt as if no man alive could throw the ball past him. Once again he picked out a fastball, whipped his wrists around, and sent a long drive sailing over the centerfielder's head. He turned on the speed, rounding first, then second. As he approached third, he saw the coach signaling for him to slide and he hit the dirt. Safe!

It was his fifth straight hit of the afternoon. But something was wrong. His right ankle was paining him. He tried to get up, but couldn't. Everyone gathered around and he was helped off the field. Irony had struck again. It was a broken ankle (Thomson's) that got him into the lineup, and now a broken ankle (his own) would take him out. Doctors operated and put a pin in the ankle, then told him to take the rest of the year off.

So Henry sat on the sidelines and watched his team finish third to the Giants and Dodgers. But he had certainly produced in his rookie season. He played in 122 games, collected 131 hits, belted 13 homers, and drove home 69 runs. His batting average was a solid

.280. One sportswriter, in fact, noted just how solid it was.

"Some .280 hitters get there by batting .450 against the worst pitchers in the league and doing next to nothing against the good ones," the man said. "Then there are the tough .280 hitters, men like Tommy Henrich and Pee Wee Reese, who get important hits against the important pitchers and tough teams. And that's just what Aaron did in his rookie season."

It was quite a compliment to the young star, but Hank himself wasn't quite satisfied.

"I'm happy I got a chance to play in the big leagues," he said, "but I feel I should have done better on the field."

Then someone reminded him of the year he had, adding that he had done better than many baseball greats in their first years. Players like Ty Cobb, Rogers Hornsby and Willie Mays hadn't hit as well as Henry in their rookie seasons.

"Maybe," Henry replied. "But I look at it this way. I've been hitting .340 all my life. I was hitting well over .400 with the Indianapolis Clowns. So hitting .280 with the Braves doesn't make me feel as if I've done my best."

When Hank reported to the Braves training camp the next year, his ankle was completely healed. And there was a surprise waiting for him. Hanging in his locker was uniform number "44." He had worn the number "5" his rookie year, but expressed a liking for double numbers, and the club decided to make the young slugger happy. He was now "44," and he'd wear that number for a long time.

Henry really began to find the range in 1955. Playing in all but one game, he pounded out 189 hits, slammed 27 homers, and drove in 106 runs. He also led the league in doubles with 37 and batted over .300 for the first time at .314. And at midseason he had participated in his first all-star game, held at Milwaukee that year. He thrilled the home fans with two singles in two trips, driving home one run. And he has played in the midsummer classic every year since.

There was one thing that dampened the 1955 season. The Braves finished second to the Dodgers in the National League race. Reporting to spring training before the 1956 season, Henry and his teammates were determined to take the pennant.

A newsman tells a funny story about Hank in 1956. It's said that he reported to spring training that year, pulled on an old uniform, borrowed a bat from someone and stepped into the cage for his first swings. He went after the first three pitches and drove each one into the distant stands.

Seeing that, he yawned, stepped out of the box, discarded the bat and drawled, "Ol' Hank is ready."

Well, "Ol' Hank" was all of 22 years old then, although he conserved his energy like a man of 40.

The 1956 season turned into one of frustration for all the Braves. When it was over, Milwaukee had held the lead for 126 days, the Dodgers for just 17. But the Brooklyn team held it when it counted, on the last day of the season, and the Braves were second-best once again. Even the Milwaukee owners were running out of patience. Toward the end of the year they fired Charlie Grimm and replaced him with tough Fred Haney. They wanted it all in '57, and wanted it badly.

Hammerin' Hank had another fine year in 1956, leading the league in hitting with a .328 mark, stroking 26 homers, and driving home 92 runs. He also topped the N.L. in hits with 200, doubles with 34, and total bases with 340. He was the real thing, all right, and quickly becoming a star.

Since the Braves moved from Boston to Milwaukee in 1954, the city had been on a baseball bender. The fans whirled through the turnstiles in County Stadium at a breakneck pace, more than two million paying their way into the park during 1956. And they watched exciting baseball. Aside from Aaron, the team had a pair of 20-game winners in Spahn and Burdette, more slugging from Ed Mathews and Joe Adcock, and played a generally superior brand of ball. Only no pennant.

In fact, Hank himself admitted after the 1956 season that for the first time in his life it really hurt him to lose.

Everyone on the team worked hard in spring training. It seemed to pay. Milwaukee won nine of its first 10 games in 1957 and jumped out in front. But a slump caught the team off guard and by mid-June dictated some changes. The result was a trade that

31

brought veteran second baseman Red Schoendienst to the Braves from the Giants.

Schoendienst gave the team its final link. A switch-hitting leader, the Redhead was a smooth fielder and tough hitter from either side of the plate. When he came to the Braves, manager Haney put him in the second spot in the lineup. The incumbent second hitter was moved into the fourth spot. His name: Hank Aaron.

The addition of Schoendienst and shifting of Hank to the cleanup spot proved an elixir for the team. They began winning again and surged back into first place. Later in the season centerfielder Bruton was hurt. Haney asked Hank if he'd mind moving to center. The youngster said he'd give it a try, and made the switch without difficulty. He was a versatile, all-around player.

Milwaukee kept getting closer and closer. On the night of September 23, 1957, the Braves were playing the Cardinals with a chance to clinch the pennant. The game was tied after nine, and was still tied when Henry came to bat in the 11th inning. He was facing a pitcher named Billy Muffet and there was one man on base.

As usual, Henry looked relaxed at the plate. But when he got a pitch he liked, he whipped his bat around and sent a towering drive out toward center. It kept carrying deeper and deeper and finally sailed out of the park for a home run. The Braves had won the National League pennant. Henry was hoisted onto the shoulders of his teammates and paraded around the field for the screaming, cheering fans. The entire city erupted in the frenetic celebration. And Hank Aaron called it the happiest moment of his life.

He had put together his first truly super season, leading the National League in homers with 44 and RBI's with 132. His .322 batting average was also near the top of the league. When the ballots were counted after the season, Hammerin' Hank Aaron was voted the National League's Most Valuable Player. In his quiet, unassuming way, he had become a superstar.

Once the pennant celebration died down, the Braves realized they still had a World Series facing them. And they'd be meeting the powerful Yankees of New York, the tough Bronx Bombers who had a habit of spending early October beating National League opponents into submission.

The Yankee roster read like a Who's Who of baseball. Mickey Mantle, Yogi Berra, Whitey Ford, and right on down the line. They were all top ballplayers. Many people felt the Braves couldn't handle the pressure.

Ford opened the series against Warren Spahn in a battle of lefthanders. It was a warm, October afternoon at Yankee Stadium and 23-year-old Hank Aaron looked up at the crowd of 70,000 fans. He found it hard to believe that he was really there, in New York's Yankee Stadium playing in the World Series.

Neither team scored in the first four innings. A double by the Yanks' Hank Bauer got a run home in the fifth. The Bombers then pushed across two more in the sixth and led, 3-0.

The Braves finally got something going in the seventh, putting two men on with none out. And they had Henry Aaron coming up. Most Milwaukee fans thought Haney would have his star bunting. But he didn't.

Ford worked Henry for a two-strike count. Then the cagey southpaw bent a sharp curve over the outside corner. It was a called third strike. The Brave rally was nipped and the Yanks went on to win the first game, 3-1.

Later, manager Haney was asked why he didn't have Hank bunt.

"Listen," he growled, "I don't bunt, especially away from home and with my best hitter up."

It showed how much faith Haney had in his star, but it didn't win the ballgame. For the second game, Haney named his righthanded ace, Lew Burdette, to oppose the Yankees' Bobby Shantz.

Hank came up to lead off the second inning. He went after a low fastball and hit a long smash to center. Mantle stood in his tracks for a second, not sure where the ball was going to come down. When he realized it was sailing, he started back, but couldn't reach it. Aaron was standing on third by the time Mantle returned the ball to the infield. A single by Adcock brought him home and the Braves led, 1-0.

The Yanks tied it in the second, but after that it was all Milwaukee, as the Braves went on to win, 4-2, with Burdette outstanding on the mound. Now the team looked forward to game three at Milwaukee.

Unfortunately, the homecoming in Milwaukee proved to be a disaster. The Brave pitchers were wild, walking 11 Yankees during the course of the game. The New Yorkers scored three runs in the first inning, two in the third, and two more in the fourth. It was a 7-1 game when Hank came up with one man on base in the fifth.

He was facing big righthander Don Larsen. Hank waited patiently. Larsen threw a fastball and he snapped his strong wrists. The ball flew off his bat, a high, deep drive to left. He watched it drop into the stands for his first World Series homer. It felt good, but the Yanks still led, 7-3.

When the Bombers erupted for five more in the seventh, it was over, a big, 12-3, victory, and a 2-1 Yankee lead in the series. Now the Braves *had* to win game four.

The Yanks took a 1-0 lead in the first inning of that encounter and it began to look bleak. But in the fourth, the Braves got moving. Shortstop Johnny Logan walked, followed by an Ed Mathews double to right. With runners on second and third, Henry stepped in, facing Yankee righthander Tom Sturdivant. The righty threw his favorite pitch, the knuckleball, but Henry was ready. He slammed the flutter pitch into the leftfield seats for another home run, putting the Braves in front, 3-1. The big man had come through again.

35

But the Yanks weren't finished. An Elston Howard home run tied the game in the ninth, and they pushed across a run in the 10th to lead it, 5-4. Then Eddie Mathews saved the Braves with a dramatic 10th-inning homer to give Milwaukee a 7-5 victory and tie the series once more.

The fifth game was an epic pitchers' battle, Burdette squaring off against Ford. Both hurlers were great and neither team could score in the early innings. Then in the last of the sixth, Mathews got an infield hit with two out. Henry wanted to keep the rally going. He swung lightly at an outside curve and blooped a single to right. When Joe Adcock singled to center, the Braves had a run. Burdette made it stand up. Milwaukee won, 1-0, and had a 3-2 lead in the series.

It was back to New York for game six. With another capacity crowd at the Stadium, the Yanks held a 2-1 lead going into the seventh inning. Henry led it off against Bullet Bob Turley. As usual, Turley fired a fastball, and Henry hit it out twice as fast as it had come in. All the way out. It was his third homer and it tied the ballgame.

But once again the hit was wasted. Hank Bauer blasted one for the Bombers in the same inning and the Yanks held on to win, 3-2. The series was tied again, and now it was a winner-take-all, one-game proposition. It would be Burdette pitching for the third time, and facing Don Larsen of the Yankees.

In the third inning, the Braves broke the ice. A

two-run double by Mathews chased Larsen, and Aaron greeted reliever Bobby Shantz with a base hit to score Mathews. Another single and subsequent ground out brought Henry home with run number four.

Henry jumped on home plate with both feet. He knew the Yanks would not catch them now, and he was right. Catcher Del Crandall belted a homer in the eighth and Burdette pitched his second straight shutout as the Braves won, 5-0. They were champions of the baseball world.

Lew Burdette was the Braves' pitching star, and the best hitter in the series was Henry Aaron. He had shown the baseball world that he was a real star. With the pressure on, Hammerin' Hank had 11 hits in seven games, just one short of the series record. He batted .393, and led both teams with three homers and seven runs batted in. It was the highspot of his career thus far.

By that time, Hank Aaron had become one of the most feared hitters in the National League. And the pitchers' suggestions on how to handle him ranged from the ridiculous to the sublime.

One veteran N.L. pitcher, who preferred to remain anonymous, said, "Aaron doesn't swing at his pitch, he swings at *our* pitch. He'll hit anything you throw at him."

Pirate star Vern Law confirmed that diagnosis. "Yeah, that's right," said Law. "My manager suggested I start him with a knuckleball, a pitch I only use after

I've set a hitter up for it. So I started Hank with a knuckleball, and he quickly started the scoring with a home run."

Don Newcombe, the veteran ace of the Dodgers, had a better idea. "How do I pitch Aaron?" repeated big Newk. "I'll tell you, I wish I could throw the ball under the plate!"

And the Giants' Sal "The Barber" Maglie had a more direct approach, one which most pitchers would be hesitant to admit. "The only way I could work Aaron," said Sal, "would be to get his face in the dirt. Then he might be edgy and I could try to finesse him. Not always, but sometimes. But the new knock-down rule is helping a hitter like him." That rule provided for an automatic $50 fine for any pitcher throwing the brushback or knockdown deliberately. It took away one of The Barber's favorite weapons.

In other words, Henry was a free swinger with extraordinary bat control. He had no pattern to his hitting. Pitchers could never tell what he would do, what pitches he would take, which ones he'd go after. He had an unusually small number of walks each season, especially for a slugger, and that, too, attested to his fondness for swinging the bat.

Some baseball purists criticized Henry for not taking more walks from overly cautious pitchers trying to work around him. With characteristic nonchalance, Hank threw off the criticism with a quick phrase. "I'd rather hit," he said, shrugging his shoulders.

Hit he did, to the tune of a .326 average in 1958, as

the Braves took their second straight pennant. Once again they faced the Yanks in the series. The Braves won the first game, 4-3, as Henry had the tying double in the eighth. He had two more hits as the Braves won the second game, 13-5.

But the Yanks won the third, 4-0, before the Braves came back behind Spahn to win the fourth, 3-0. Hank had two more hits in that one and Milwaukee led, three games to one. It looked as if they'd repeat as champs.

Only this time the team lacked the knockout punch. Bob Turley shut out the Braves in game five, 7-0, and the Yanks took the sixth one in 10 innings, 4-3. It was a one-game series again, with a rematch of Lew Burdette and Don Larsen. Neither was around at the end, the Yanks winning it, 6-2, with Turley the pitching star in relief.

It was a great comeback win for the Yankees and a bitter disappointment for the Braves. Henry had nine hits for a .333 average, but he didn't hit the long ball, with no homers and just two RBI's. It was one of the few times he wasn't the dominant man with the stick.

The next year saw the beginning of the end of the Milwaukee dynasty. The team fought all year long, but was tied by the Dodgers at the end. In a playoff for the pennant, the Los Angeles team won in two straight games and Milwaukee was finished. A disgruntled Aaron said sadly:

"We lost on the last day of the season in 1956," he

said, "and in a playoff in 1959. With a little more luck, we could have won four straight pennants."

Henry was truly a team player. He was saddened by the team's playoff loss. Completely ignored was his own personal season, by far the best since he had come into the league.

He came out of the gate swinging as usual, only this time he was making better contact than ever. By mid-May, the time when most players' averages begin to level off, Henry was still belting the ball at a .468 clip. It made everyone in baseball stop and take notice.

One writer said that it was Aaron, not Mays or Mantle, who was now the logical successor to Stan Musial and Ted Williams as the next great hitter in baseball. And the great Hall of Famer, Rogers Hornsby, claimed that Aaron was the only major leaguer with a reasonable chance to hit .400.

"With those wrists," said the Rajah, "Aaron can be fooled a little and still hit the hell out of the ball."

Hank's manager, Fred Haney, agreed. "Henry is capable of hitting .400, but don't forget, it takes luck as well as ability. The hits have to drop in all year long."

"There are other factors, too," he continued. "In my day, we played at the same time, day in and day out. There were no night games, of course. We ate more regularly and we had easier trips. We didn't have to go cross country all the time.

"Today, a ballplayer might play a tough night game and have to be out on the field the next afternoon, ready to go again. The next day's pitcher can go home early during a night game, but the hitters have to hang around. I think the irregularity of the game hurts the hitter, and that's one of the biggest reasons that it's tougher to hit .400 now."

But for the first time in his career, Henry was badgered by reporters, asking the same questions over and over.

"Can you hit .400 Hank?"

"Do you think you'll crack .400?"

"How's .400 looking, Henry?"

He had to work to develop a defense mechanism. Sometimes he was blunt. One reporter asked about .400 and Hank said, "I don't like to talk about that." Another asked him about his immediate hitting goal, hoping to get into a discussion of a .400 season. But he replied, "Right now I want two more hits. That'll give me 1,000 and I'll be just 2,000 behind Musial."

So Hammerin' Hank was fighting the pressures. It's hard to say whether that got to him or whether it was the intangibles of the long season that Fred Haney mentioned, but his average gradually dropped below .400. Yet he avoided any kind of prolonged slump. It's just that there was such great expectation from the start he had that many people voiced disappointment when .400 seemed no longer probable.

It didn't affect Henry's basic, relaxed style. Someone asked the veteran Philly star, Robin Roberts, about pitching to a hot Aaron and Robin replied, "How can you fool Aaron? He falls asleep between pitches."

It wasn't really that way. Henry himself admitted that he forced himself to relax at the plate. "I'm as tense as the next guy, but you can't hit if you're tight. I make myself relax up there, concentrate on it. I'm not always as casual as most people think. It takes practice to relax."

The 1959 season ended with the playoff loss to the Dodgers. But Henry had done his best. He led the league in hitting for the second time with an eye-popping .355 average. In addition, he topped the N.L. in hits with 223 and in total bases with 400. And his 39 home runs and 123 RBI's weren't totals compiled by a nickel-and-dime hitter. Henry Aaron was simply devastating.

Henry might not have realized it at the time, but he was carrying a bigger load than ever before. The Brave players who had been in their prime when Henry first came up were now becoming aging veterans, who didn't produce at the same high level that they once had. It was a fact of baseball life. The team was moving into a period of decline.

During the next three seasons, Henry continued to play great, all-around baseball. He hit 40, 34 and 45 home runs, driving in 126, 120 and 128 runs during that time. He was under .300 in 1960 (.292), but bounced back for .327 and .323 marks the next two years. Henry was still tops, but the Braves weren't.

The team even had a new manager, Bobby Bragan, a cagey baseball veteran who liked to get the most out of his players. When he talked to Henry, there wasn't much he could criticize, but he did see one area for improvement.

"You're a complete ballplayer," he told the superstar. "But you're not using all your talents. I think you should run the bases more."

When the Braves won the pennant in 1957, the year Henry was the league's Most Valuable Player, he had only stolen one base. With Bragan at the helm starting in 1960, he swiped 16, 21 and 15 over the next three seasons. As usual, when Henry decided to do something on a baseball field, he was quite adept at it. The Braves still had a slugging team, so Henry didn't run all that much. But when he did, he was as good as they come.

In 1963, Hank was the National League's Player of the Year. He had another fantastic all-around season. During that year he became just the fifth man in baseball history to hit more than 30 homers (he had 44) and steal more than 30 bases (he stole 31) in the same season. He led the league in homers again as well as in RBI's with 130 and hits with 201, and also in total bases. His batting average was .319. It was already his tenth season in the big leagues.

The next two seasons were not great ones by Henry's usual standards. He hit .328 and .318, but his run production was off somewhat. Nevertheless, he was still one of the few bright spots on the Braves. The great following in Milwaukee was built around the personalities of the ballplayers. Spahn, Burdette, Mathews, Adcock, Logan, Crandall, Covington. Now they were all fading, or already gone. Players were coming and going, and so were managers. The team was losing its personality and the fans were losing the desire to attend the games.

It was a sad situation, because for almost a decade, Milwaukee had been the hottest baseball town in the country. Now the seats were increasingly empty and the team owners decided they had to do something about it. After the 1965 season, it was announced that the team would be moving to Atlanta, Georgia. The move was greeted with mixed emotions by some of the players. The Braves would be the first big league team to play in the south. Some worried about the treatment the black players would receive.

As it turned out, there was no problem. Henry liked the new ballpark. The ball seemed to carry there, and in his first season he promptly walloped 44 homers and drove in 127 runs. But his batting average was a career low .279.

"I don't really know what happened," he said. "I guess I wanted to hit the long ball for the new fans. I know I'm not a .279 hitter. I'll have the average back up next year."

The low average bothered Henry more than anything else. He did reach a couple of milestones that year. On April 20, he hit the 400th homer of his career off Bo Belinsky of Philadelphia. And later in the year, he and teammate Eddie Mathews set a record for the most home runs hit by two players on the same team. They would hit 863 before Mathews was traded, and the men who held the record before the two Braves were a couple of guys named Ruth and Gehrig.

To show their appreciation for his long contributions to the team, the Braves awarded Hank a two-year contract prior to the 1967, calling for $100,000 per season. It was about time. Other superstars were making that much, and Henry Aaron was certainly as good as any of them. In addition, he was an immediate favorite with the Atlanta fans. They cheered loud and long every time he came to the plate. And he responded with some very candid comments about his baseball past.

"I guess you could say I was a lost cause in Milwaukee," he admitted. "I was always in the shadows of Burdette, Spahn and Mathews. They were the big boys, even after that big year I had in '57."

So Henry was glad to be in Atlanta. He made good on his promise to get over the .300 mark by hitting .307 in 1967. He still found time to belt another 39 homers and drive in 109 runs. He was as consistent as the sun. The next year, he belted number 500 off Mike McCormick of the Giants. Now he was entering a class reserved for the likes of Mays and Mantle. And he was enjoying every minute of it. At the age of 34, he was finding a second childhood in Atlanta.

"I can't remember getting an ovation like that one when I hit my 500th homer," he said. "And I'm glad I got it off a pitcher like McCormick. It always makes

45

it nicer when you do something like that off one of the best."

Some of the other so-called best also had things to say about Hank Aaron, all of it full of respect and admiration.

Said Sandy Koufax, the great flame-throwing left-hander of the Dodgers, "He's the toughest in the league. There's no way you can pitch him when he's hot."

Giants' star hurler Juan Marichal said it another way after Henry ripped him for four hits and two stolen bases. "That man," said Juan, "if he doesn't beat you one way, he beats you another."

And a journeyman catcher named Charlie Lau, who had played in both leagues, complimented Henry this way:

"I've seen every superstar of recent years—Mantle, Mays, Kaline, Mathews, Clement, all of them—and Aaron's the best. He beats you hitting, running, fielding and stealing. There's nothing he can't do."

Even the great Mickey Mantle looked upon Henry as a very special breed of ballplayer. "As far as I'm concerned," said the Mick, "Henry Aaron is the best ballplayer of my era. He is to baseball of the last 15 years what Joe DiMaggio was before him."

Quite a tribute from a man who always outshone Hammerin' Hank in the public eye. But Henry was finally getting his due. As the records began to fall, reporters and newsmen began approaching him with increased regularity, asking him about this mark and that record. To them, Henry would reply:

"Setting records means you're getting old."

The Braves were aware of his age, too. Although Hank had been in remarkably good health, the team didn't want to take any chances. They began resting him during one game of doubleheaders, and letting him sit out a few day games that followed night games. He also played some first base to save his legs, taking to the new position with his usual style and grace.

For the past several seasons, the Braves' big problem had been pitching. The team always seemed to have enough lumber, but not enough arms. In 1969, they got the right combination going to take the National League's Western Division title. Under the new divisional setup, they had to meet the Eastern Division winner, the New York Mets, to get into the World Series.

Henry made his usual contribution, batting an even .300, belting 44 more homers, and driving in 97 runs. He played in 147 games, indicating how the Braves were resting him.

Atlanta was highly optimistic going into the playoffs, but 1969 was the year of the Mets and nothing was about to stop the New Yorkers. They took three straight from the Braves, despite a home run by Hank Aaron in each game. He did his best to avert defeat, but the Met steamroller was just too much.

In 1970, Henry reached another milestone. He collected his 3,000th base hit, becoming just the ninth man in baseball history to do it. After the game, he told reporters:

"That's what I've always wanted. Now that I have 3,000 hits, everything else will fall into place—the homers, runs batted in, everything. This has meant a lot to me."

Now, more than ever before, people wanted to know about Hank Aaron. While Mays' and Mantle's every move had been relayed to the public for two decades, Henry still toiled in relative obscurity. *The Quiet Legend, The Neglected Superstar, The Quiet Slugger:* these were some of the ways people had referred to Henry over the years. Now, with records falling like trees in a lumber camp, people wanted to know more.

Someone once asked a team official why Henry wasn't more of a holler guy on the field.

"Henry might not be the big back-slapper and talker," the man said, "but he's the real head around here. Everyone on the team has tremendous respect for him. But he's so quiet and so modest that you've got to watch him closely for a long while before you fully realize what a deep influence he has.

"The young players are always watching Henry. They scrutinize his every move, how he swings, how he reacts to different pitchers, how he moves. And he's never too busy to answer any questions they have about all phases of the game and about their personal problems as well.

"And Henry's a good listener. He's always ready to laugh at a joke, making a young guy feel wanted. He creates a whole kind of family mood around here and it's especially valuable when the team isn't going too well. He's a take-charge guy with deeds rather than words, a leader by example."

Henry himself was also beginning to reveal more in his interviews with the press. Early in his career he was very restrained, almost distrustful of reporters. But now, with his status as baseball's elder statesman, he feels he can speak his piece on a variety of topics.

He talked about matters directly related to the game. "An intelligent player is always thinking on the field. Even in the outfield, I watch everything. For instance, on a 3-2 pitch, I'll assume a guy like Nash is going to try to slip a fastball by a hitter like Doug Rader. So I'll edge over to the line a bit, guessing that Doug will go with the pitch late to rightfield."

Ten years earlier, some people thought that Aaron was so relaxed in the outfield that he just ambled around between pitches. They never realized the subtle position changes he was making.

He also talked about baseball-related topics, such as the need for a black manager in the majors. "I think I know enough about the game and about how to get along with a whole team to produce a winner," he said. "So do Ernie (Banks) and Willie (Mays). Unfortunately, no owner has yet had the common sense to hire a black manager. I don't even call it guts, I call it common sense. It's already been proven in

49

baseball that a black man can produce a winner and bring in sellout crowds.

"Now there are certain white managers, guys like Alston and Hodges, who should be hired and rehired, because they've proved they can work with players and they know how to get the most out of a team. But then there's another group of guys who have failed here and failed there. Yet they keep getting rehired by other clubs. It just doesn't seem right."

Back on the ballfield, Henry was still a potent force. At 37, he put together one of the most remarkable seasons ever for a man of his age. On April 27, 1971, Henry stood at home plate facing wily Gaylord Perry of the Giants.

Perry has always been known as a man who might load the baseball. Whether he threw the illegal spitter or not was immaterial. Whatever he threw, Henry hit it hard. The ball sailed deep to left and cleared the wall. It was the 600th home run of his career. He continued to powder the ball the rest of the year. The Braves weren't really going anywhere, but Henry still got himself up for the game day after day.

When the season ended, Henry had played in 139 games, the fewest since his rookie year of 1954. But his 162 hits were good for a .327 batting average. He finished the year with 639 homers, just seven behind Mays, who was three years older at 40 and seemingly near the end of the line.

Despite the publicity and talk of Henry's assault on the Babe, the Atlanta slugger continued to live a quiet private life. He and his wife have a modest home in Atlanta and spend quite a bit of time enjoying their four children.

Shortly before the start of the 1972 season, the Braves announced that Henry Aaron had signed a contract calling for $200,000 per year. It made him the highest paid player in baseball history. After years of playing in shadows, Henry Aaron was finally getting his due.

"He deserves every penny of it," proclaimed Braves' president Bill Bartholomay.

He was right. More and more people will be coming out to watch Hank Aaron as he begins his final countdown. He showed little signs of slipping in 1972, although his totals were below his outstanding 1971 season. But he still managed 34 homers while playing in just 129 games. He was being rested more and more. Among his 119 hits were 77 RBI's, putting him into second place on the all-time list behind Babe Ruth. His 231 total bases enabled him to pass Stan Musial and become the all-time leader in that department. And his total of 673 homers left him just 41 behind the Babe.

The only area in which he slipped was batting average, coming in with a .265 mark, well below his .312 lifetime figure. But that may indicate his growing consciousness about home runs.

"I'm not as strong a hitter as I was once," Henry said recently. "When I won the home run title with 44 in 1957, a lot of my shots were to rightfield. Now I pull everything to left. I guess I was a better hitter then."

Yet Henry has shown no discernible diminishing of skills, and someone once asked him how an athlete of his age and with his longevity in the game could continue to perform at the same level of excellence as he had 10 or 15 years earlier.

He replied: "I don't know if it's a conscious thing or not, but the knowledge of age is definitely somewhere in the back of your mind. You're aware that one bad year, or even a bad month or bad week will have everyone talking about how you're slipping. So you put out more, give something extra, not just for those watching you, but for your own sake, too. It would be awful not to do justice to a talent that you've taken pride in and dedicated yourself to for your whole life."

So with that attitude, a very positive one, Henry reported to spring training for the 1973 season. He was aware of the pressure he'd be facing as the official countdown began. Yet with his calm attitude, pressure had never bothered him before and he didn't think it would get to him now.

"First of all, I don't think I'll approach the record this year," he told the press early in the season. "I don't play the full schedule this year and there just may not be enough at-bats to do it. I'm not really expecting to break the record this season, but I should get close enough to have plenty of time next season. So I'm really not worried."

Then a strange thing happened. Henry started the

1973 season in a horrendous batting slump—in all respects but one. He was hitting home runs. Five of his first seven hits were homers, and since he was batting under .200, many people began to accuse him of being homer-happy, of disregarding his team role and just shooting for the record. But they should have known that Henry Aaron doesn't operate that way.

"It's just one of those things," Hank said. "Sure, I pull the ball more than I did when I was young, but I'm not consciously going for homers. And I'm not worried, either. I may not be a .300 hitter anymore, but the hits will come, believe me."

They did, but not very fast. Hank climbed slowly to .210, then .220. It appeared to many that he might not have enough left to hit .250. But the homers continued to come, and he remained up among the league leaders. It amazed people that the 39-year-old Aaron could still get his bat around against the strong pitching arms prevalent in the league. Physically, Hank seemed about as strong as always. His weight was never a problem and even the knee that had bothered him for several seasons showed no signs of worsening. A touch of arthritis in his neck and shoulders prompted Manager Mathews to move him from right to left field, because a leftfielder doesn't have the same number of long, hard throws to home and third. And Henry's throwing had slipped.

But it was his hitting, in other words his homers, that everyone was interested in. It was becoming Aaron's race a lot sooner than the fans had thought it would. There was hardly a ripple when Henry passed the great Stan Musial as the all-time total bases leader during the season. Everyone was too busy counting down to the Babe. The statisticians had a field day.

Ever since the Braves moved to Atlanta, it has been pointed out that the stadium there is an easy park to hit in. They call it "the launching pad." The dimensions are not great and the double-tiered stands all around keep away damaging wind currents. It is the perfect home base for someone trying to break the home-run record.

But what if the Braves hadn't moved, what if they remained in Milwaukee and Hank had to finish his career there? That was just one question the statisticians played with during the year.

Early in the '73 season a report was issued stating that Hank had played 586 games in Atlanta, and hit 162 homers for an average of one per every 3.61 games played. In Milwaukee, Hank had played 940 games, hitting 185 homers for an average of one per every 5.08 games. In little Wrigley Field (home of the Chicago Cubs), another hitting park, Henry had played 178 games, hitting 48 homers for one per every 3.75 games.

The report concluded that if Hank had played his entire career in Atlanta, his homer total would have been 761, way above the Babe. If he had been a Cub and played at Wrigley Field, it would have been 751. But, conversely, had the Braves not moved from Milwaukee, Henry would have only been around the 640 mark and probably wouldn't make it.

Of course, statistics don't always take account of variables. Henry improved as a hitter in his later years and who's to say that his homer totals wouldn't have escalated in Milwaukee, too. And don't forget, Babe Ruth played at Yankee Stadium, known for its short rightfield wall that always favored the Yanks' lefthanded powerhitters.

Some purists also liked to point out that Henry has had almost 3,000 more at-bats in his career than the Babe, and that he was averaging only 6.3 homers per 100 at-bats, as compared to 10.5 for Ruth. The answer to that is that Henry didn't become a pull hitter until five years ago, while Ruth was a home run hitter throughout his career. In the past five years alone, Henry's average has been 10.5 homers per 100 at-bats.

Then someone pointed out that Babe's lifetime batting average was .342, 30-odd points higher than Hank's .309. But you can always answer stats with stats. Modernists claim there is better pitching today, as indicated by a league average of around .280 in Ruth's day compared to an average of around .250 today. So that dispute was a standoff.

There were other comparisons. Cincy outfielder Pete Rose loved to study the old time ballplayers since he plays like many of them. Pete considered himself an authority on the Babe, and he volunteered his own comparison between Ruth and Aaron.

"I feel as if I know the Babe," said Rose. "He was

great, all right, but so is Henry. And don't forget, Ruth never played night ball or traveled the way we do. There wasn't as much physical strain on him."

A good case can be made for Rose's statement. Experts have said all along that it's more difficult to play ball at night. After all, only the top half of the ball is illuminated. The bottom half is dark. As for travel, psychologists have always maintained that riding in an airplane is much more wearing than traveling by train. And the Braves are in the National League's Western Division, necessitating long trips to the west coast, to Houston, the midwest, and the east coast. It's a fact that the Braves travel some 30,000 miles more per year than any other team in either league. As one writer put it:

"The wear and tear on Henry Aaron is greater than it has been on any other great hitter!"

When all the facts are gathered together, it seems impossible to say that either Hank or the Babe had a distinct advantage over the other. The plusses and minuses seem to balance out. Henry fully deserves all the credit and the accolades that go with tremendous achievement.

Oddly enough, Babe Ruth liked the same bat that Hank prefers. Though the Babe used a much heavier model, their bats are of almost identical proportion. And since the models are named for the player who designs them, Hank actually used a Ruth model for several years early in his career.

By mid-May of 1973, Hank had 11 home runs

though his average was still in the low .200's. About that time, another phenomenon began to appear—it was "hate mail." A growing number of letters came to Hank in many forms, shapes, and sizes, but all bearing the same message. They were violently opposed to a black man breaking Babe Ruth's record, and they contained racial slurs of the worst kind. The majority of these letters came not from the south but from large cities in the north.

"Right now the mail is running some 75-25 against me," Hank admitted in a candid press conference. "Most of it is racial. They call me 'nigger' and every other bad word you can imagine. If I was white, all America would be proud of me. As far as I'm concerned, it indicates something very low in this country."

Henry was angry, and understandably so. In addition, he was beginning to hear the same kind of flak from the stands in several ballparks, including his own at Atlanta. One time he even threatened to go into the stands after an obviously drunken spectator who wouldn't let up on him.

"Most of the fans are fine," Hank said. "I don't care if they boo me. They paid their money to get in and they're entitled to it. But I won't take the racial stuff. I don't have to. But I'll tell you one thing. All this is just making me more determined than ever to break the record."

Braves officials were equally alarmed by the situation. "We've got to be concerned about this," said Donald Davidson, assistant to Braves president Bill Bartholomay. "We know it's bothering Hank. It has to. And recent history has shown us that there are a lot of crazy people running around this country and you don't know what they're liable to do."

The Braves asked for special policemen in each city to escort Hank to and from the team bus and whenever he was in public view. He was given special, protected hotel suites, sometimes away from the rest of the team. The special treatment bothered and embarrassed him, but he knew it was necessary.

Although the hate mail only represented a small part of the population—the cranks and crackpots—it began getting coast-to-coast publicity and served to wake up many people who didn't realize what was happening. When Hank said,

"What do they expect me to do, stop hitting home runs?" people's sympathies were aroused. Suddenly, the hate-mail started dropping off, apparently having run its course, and letters of support by the hundreds began pouring into Atlanta from all over the land. The whole atmosphere changed and it made Hank very happy.

Toward the end of the season, political pollster Louis Harris decided to take a special Harris Sports Survey to see how the American public really felt about Henry Aaron. The results were gratifying.

First of all, the poll showed that only nine percent of all Americans hoped Hank wouldn't break the record. Another 18 percent didn't care either way, and the rest, some 73 percent, were pulling for him to make it.

Most people agreed that no matter where Hank finished, his achievements certainly wouldn't hurt the memory of the Babe. Ruth would always be the Sultan of Swat, a legend. And some 87.5 percent agreed that "Hank Aaron has been a great player for years and it will be good to see him get his due recognition when he breaks the lifetime home run record." The same people agreed that above all Henry was a gentleman and a credit to the sport.

The poll also helped show how small the proportion of hate mail writers was. A 63-26 margin were "shocked to hear people are rooting against Aaron because he is black." And over 90 percent agreed that it was "foolish to choose between Babe Ruth and Hank Aaron because both have been great baseball players." And finally, the poll showed that more people were interested in and following baseball in 1973, partly because of Hank's assault on the record.

And that assault was getting more interesting. By mid-July Hank was bearing down on the 700 mark. His average was still around .250, but the homers came with a regularity surprising for a player his age. In fact, he was still up with the league leaders, battling the likes of Willie Stargell and Bobby Bonds for the homer lead. When he cracked number 700 off Ken Brett of the Phillies on July 21, everyone took notice.

The homer was his 27th of the season, a figure many people thought he'd have trouble reaching over the entire year. And it was only the third week of July; he still had more than two months to get the additional 15 homers he needed for the record. It was going to be close.

Atlanta began getting ready. About 20 large billboards were erected around the city, each one reading . . . ATLANTA SALUTES . . . and showing a large portrait of Hank swinging a bat. Each board would light up with the current homer number and could be seen for miles around.

In addition, cash prizes were being offered for the return of the homerun baseballs from number 700 on. For instance, the person retrieving homer 701 would get 701 silver dollars. To prevent any fraud, whenever Hank came to bat a special baseball was used with a marking that would show up under a certain kind of light. So Hank was really causing excitement all around the league.

The kind of season Henry was having naturally confirmed his great physical skills. But there was something else that helped him, too. The Braves were a power team. They never seriously challenged for the division title because they had poor pitching, average fielding, and a general lack of team speed. But they had the power hitters with which to surround their star.

Third baseman Darrell Evans and second sacker Dave Johnson were both running at 40-homer-season paces. Roadrunner Ralph Garr was always on base, while Dusty Baker and Mike Lum also hit with authority. So a pitcher couldn't work around Henry with any kind of assurance. He had the guns all around him so they couldn't afford to walk him.

And what about those pitchers? After all, the hurler who served up the record-breaking homer would go down in the books all right, alongside the likes of Tom Zachery, Ralph Branca, and Tracy Stallard, men remembered for giving up famous homers to the Babe (number 60), Bobby Thomson (the famous pennant-winner homer of 1951), and Roger Maris (number 61 in 1961). Statements from pitchers around the league were quite surprising.

Tug McGraw, the super relief star of the Mets, felt that the man serving up number 715 could actually work it to his advantage financially.

"The man would be a commodity," said Tug. "He'd be in demand all over the banquet circuit. If I was facing him in that situation I'd throw my best pitch and hope like hell he hits it out."

Some others went even further than McGraw. Reggie Cleveland of St. Louis said: "I'd throw a medium fastball right down the pike. If he's gonna get it off somebody, it might as well be me. Andy Messersmith of the Dodgers proclaimed: I'll lay it right in there." And Larry Dierker of the Astros stated: I think I'd throw one right down the middle just to see what happened. I wouldn't be doing it for the record book or for the money, but just for the hell of it because it seems like a crazy thing to do."

Some hurlers were indifferent, neither looking forward to it or worrying about it. "I've thrown so many homers in my career," said the Dodgers' Pete Richert, "that another wouldn't really matter. I wouldn't mind throwing the 715th." And the great Juan Marichal of the Giants said: "I've never won anything in 13½ years, nothing. If Aaron broke the record off me it would be like a trophy. It would be O.K."

Then there were those who claimed they'd try their hardest to prevent the Hammer from connecting.

Among them were Jack Billingham and Clay Carroll, both of the Cincinnati Reds. Said Billingham: "If I'm going to be remembered I want it to be for something good that I did. I don't want to leave my mark that way. As for endorsements, if there were any they'd be the kind that made you look like a jerk." Carroll's comment was short and to the point. "I don't want to be remembered that way. He'd get the endorsements; I'd be the goat."

Dave Roberts of Houston was another hurler dead set against being victim number 715. "Giving up the big homer certainly wouldn't be to the pitcher's advantage," said Roberts. There are a lot of better ways to be remembered and I'd like to try one of them. I'd rather be remembered as the guy who faced Aaron with 714 homers in his last at bat in the major leagues and stopped him from breaking the record!"

The story that carried the pitchers' comments made good reading. It amused nearly everyone, but not baseball commissioner Bowie Kuhn. He read it and did a slow burn. How dare a professional ballplayer announce publicly that he'd groove one for Aaron. It didn't take long after the story broke for Kuhn to issue a directive. It said, in effect, that any pitcher found not trying his hardest to get Henry Aaron out, no matter what the circumstance, would be subject to stiff disciplinary action. That meant a fine, perhaps suspension, maybe both. Kuhn was trying to keep baseball clean, but he was taking some of the fun out of it just the same.

Once Henry reached the 700 mark the pressure began to mount, much of it caused by outside influences, media people, well-wishers, second-guessers. They didn't leave him alone. Many wondered if Henry would suffer the same fate that the Yank's Roger Maris suffered back in 1961, the year he cracked Ruth's single-season mark: As the days dwindled down that year, it became obvious that only Maris (not teammate Mickey Mantle) had a shot at the record. From that point on Maris was completely inundated. He didn't have a moment to himself, a moment to forget what was happening to him. Never an outgoing individual, a man who always had a difficult time handling the press, he couldn't take it. Maris got the record (a tribute to him as an athelete), but he alienated many fans and media people. The emotional strain also caused him to literally lose some of the hair on his head. The entire ordeal was probably something he'd never forget, and given a choice again, he'd undoubtedly have settled for a comfortable 51 homers instead of 61.

Now Henry was beginning to come under the same kind of pressure. Starting with the hate mail and racial slurs of the early season, it developed into an intense press and media campaign as he closed in. You couldn't blame the writers, and broadcasters. They had a job to do and Henry was news. He knew it, too, and tried to keep his cool, politely answering the same questions, over and over again, in a quiet, stable, unemotional voice.

Those closest to Henry best understood the pressure he was under. Braves' publicity director Bob Hope said:

"Wherever Henry goes he's under intense, relentless pressure from the media. He gets the same questions all the time, and whenever so much is written on one subject, there are bound to be some misquotes. This really irritates him. He's always been a guy who'd talk to anyone at almost anytime. But the preponderance of misquotes have made him more guarded in his comments."

Manager Eddie Mathews was also aware of how the media chased Aaron. "You've got to remember that Henry's been in the limelight for a long time," said Mathews, "and in that respect he's used to it. So he really doesn't have a problem with the everyday working press, the guys he knows and trusts.

"The problem usually occurs with one-shot writers, guys who fly in to do a quick story and keep badgering him until they get it. It's the constant influx of strangers, each looking for his own story angle, that has made for a difficult situation."

One member of the working press who saw Henry every day was Frank Hyland of the *Atlanta Journal*. He knew just what a day in the life of Henry Aaron was like.

"All kinds of people are always trying to get to Hank," said Hyland. "Some want stories, others try to talk him into endorsements, and some offer crazy, fly-by-night schemes that only an idiot would be interested in. It's tough for Hank because he's always been a very private person and now he's lost all semblance of a private life.

"Just recently he and I were having coffee in a Cincinnati restaurant. What happened was almost unbelievable. People kept approaching him in waves, asking for autographs, shaking his hand, or just wanting to talk. We couldn't even drink our coffee, let alone carry on a conversation. We finally had to leave the restaurant.

"It's gotten to a point where Hank can't go into a public place. Even at the ballparks crowds gather everywhere waiting for him. They're right at the exit and he's literally got to fight his way to the team bus."

Then Eddie Mathews added. "Hank has always been a great team player and he still thinks of the team before anything else. But not even the players let him forget about the record. They all love being a part of it because they know it's a part of history."

And early in the season, when Henry was hitting

homers and little else, Frank Hyland noted: "Hank doesn't consciously go for homers now, but the fences must be on his mind since he hears about it so much. He told me that he'd love to be a .350 hitter again, but he can't be. He feels the home run is the best way for him to contribute."

From those who know him best to those who just barely know him, very few people have a bad thing to say about Henry Aaron. He's friendly to everyone and has never acted in any way or done any thing that could be held against him.

New York Mets star Cleon Jones is from Hank's hometown of Mobile, Alabama, and remembers Henry from way back.

"I was a batboy for the Mobile Black Bears when Henry was a teenage star there," recalls Cleon, "so I've known him for a long time. You ask me about Henry the man and I've got to call him a super, super, super human being. And this is not only on the ball field but in life in general. As big as he is he's so modest. He could walk into a place and people would never know he's there. But if one person, or two or 20 ask him for his autograph, he always signs and gives them a smile."

Henry has stood up well to the pressures. By the time Henry had his 21st home run early in July, some-one pointed out that he had only 52 total hits for the year, a remarkable homer-to-hit ratio. Was he going for home runs? And what would breaking the record mean to him? Hank answered quietly and slowly.

"Heck," he said in a soft, mocking tone. "If I stopped hitting home runs I'd stop hitting, period.

"I haven't really changed my style," he added. "It's just that when you get older you get a little bit more patient in waiting for the good pitch.

"But to tell the truth, when you're close to 40, you're at an age where the game begins to get a little dull. You start thinking about quitting, a thought that never entered your mind ten years earlier. But as for myself, with the record so close, I'd be denying myself the privilege if I didn't go for it. If I wasn't as close as I am, this would be my last year. But next year will definitely be the last."

So Hank handled those routine questions similarly all season. The only time he became angry was when someone fed him an offbeat question and badgered him into giving them an answer.

One day an insistent reporter demanded to know if Hank was taking sleeping pills to ease the pressure. Hank said no casually, then found the question repeated several more times. Finally he raised his deep baritone voice and said emphatically:

"Will you please take no for an answer. I don't use them. I don't need them!"

There were a few other signs of irritation and sensitivity induced by pressure. When he belted number 700 he refused to send the ball to the Hall of Fame, the institution that traditionally collects such symbols of famous deeds. But Henry was angry that the Hall had never acknowledged receipt of his 500th and 600th with any kind of note, any kind of thanks.

He also criticized Commissioner Kuhn for not sending him a telegram of congratulations after his 700th. It may be noted that both Kuhn and the Hall later made amends for these oversights.

On numerous occasions Henry was asked to compare the pressure on Roger Maris with that on himself.

"It was a different kind of pressure on Roger Maris," Henry would explain. "He was under a strict time limit. He had to do it before the season ended. There'd never be another chance. In a sense, I've got all the time in the world. If I don't do it this season, I'll do it next season. In other words, unless I get hit by a truck, I'll do it."

The last statement might have been made in jest, but there was a flavor of irony in it. Perhaps Henry was thinking of Roberto Clemente, perhaps not. But during the year more than a few people thought of the tragedy that took the life of the Pittsburgh star on New Years Eve of 1972. Clemente had collected his 3,000th basehit in his final at bat of the 1972 season. He didn't know it then, but it was his last at-bat ever. Had he failed to hit, he wouldn't have reached the coveted plateau.

But Henry genuinely felt he'd be back in '74 in an excellent position to break the mark almost at his leisure.

And the homers continued to come. Hank got number 698 against Tug McGraw of the Mets. But he was upset that the Braves had lost, 8-7, as the Mets scored seven times in the final inning to pull it out.

"I'd rather have us winning the pennant than have me break the record," he told the New York press as they charged him after the game.

"Henry means that," said Manager Mathews. "We won pennants in 1957 and '58, then got nothing until 1969 when we took the West title. And the Mets beat us three straight in the playoffs. Henry's always at his best when it means the most, like all great players, and it's a shame the Braves couldn't have won more often. But I can tell you that team-comes-first talk isn't just idle chatter with him. He means it."

Number 699 came on July 20, off Wayne Twitchell of Philly, the same man he had clipped for number 649 the year before, the homer that put him in front of Mays to stay. And the next day he collected his 700th and the Aaron watchers really turned it on. Then, just when it seemed as if he'd break the record by mid-September, Hank took a little vacation.

He didn't get number 701 until 10 days later, on July 31, and then another 16 days passed before he connected for 702 off Jack Aker of the Cubs. Now, instead of more than two months to hit 15 homers, he had a little more that one month to hit 13. The chances were dwindling.

"We've got 28 games left and I won't be playing in all of them," Hank said, after connecting off Aker. "So I don't think it's really possible anymore for me this

69

year. I haven't been swinging good the last couple of weeks and I've really had to concentrate on getting my timing back.

"I wasn't thinking home run when I faced Aker, but he tossed a high fastball down the middle and I connected. It was probably the hardest ball I've hit in almost three weeks. It's always good to come in to Wrigley Field for a few games."

The homer off Aker started Hank on another good streak. He got number 703 the next day against Steve Renko of Montreal and 704 the day after that off Steve Rogers of the Expos. That made four straight homers off righthanded pitchers since his 700th off Brett.

Number 705 came on August 22, off Reggie Cleveland of St. Louis and 706 followed on the 28th, this one off Milt Pappas of the Cubs. So entering September, Henry needed nine homers to break the record. The good streak had incidentally taken his batting average into the mid-.260's, the highest point it had been all year.

And the guessing game continued. Would he or wouldn't he? Hank had never hit many homers in September, but he was hitting well and that was a good sign. On September 3, he belted two long homers in the same game against the San Diego Padres. That made the count 708. He wasn't going to give up the chase without a fight, telling people he'd love to go over the top in '73.

Number 709 followed on the eighth, off Jack Billingham of Cincinnati, and two days later he got 710, this one off Don Carrithers of the Giants. That drive came in the third inning and it not only gave him another homer, but raised his overall batting average to .288, a remarkable figure in view of the fact that many people believed Henry wouldn't hit much over .240 for the year.

But there was an ominous sign, too. An inning after he hit his homer, Henry suddenly and unexpectedly left the game. Fans in Atlanta wondered if it were just a rest. But Henry usually didn't leave a game that way, especially after he'd hit a homer and appeared in a good groove. After the game, Manager Mathews told the press what happened.

"Hank was removed from the game because of severe stomach cramp. We took him to a doctor as a precaution and have just received word that everything is O.K. Nothing to worry about and he shouldn't miss any time."

Although Hank was two for two, with a homer and pair of RBI's when he went out, the press jumped on the story. Hank's nerves are shot, they said.

"It wasn't nerves," said teammate Dave Johnson. "Hank's been having a bit of stomach trouble lately but I think it's from something he ate. I wouldn't blame him if it were his nerves, but I'm sure it isn't."

Johnson was right. Hank returned to action, but it took another week for him to connect again, this time in Atlanta. In the eighth inning against San Diego righthander Gary Ross, Hank got around on an 0-1 fastball and lined it just inside the leftfield foul pole. He trotted out number 711, to the cheers of just 1,362 patrons. It was an all-time low for Atlanta, and with baseball history in the making, was a source of embarrassment for the city.

"It's kind of a weird thing," said a high city official. "The whole town's talking about Hank, but they just don't turn out to the ballpark. Maybe it's racial to some extent, but the main reason, I think, is that this is still primarily a football city. The Falcons (Atlanta's NFL team) fill the stadium every Sunday, win, lose, or draw."

The reasons for the paltry attendance aren't clear. They can't be all racial, since Atlanta is now slightly more than 50 percent black and not even the blacks were turning out. While Atlanta is a football-city, the Falcons play just seven home games a year to the Braves 81. Perhaps the main reason is that no one likes a loser. The team, with the exception of Henry, just wasn't exciting enough and was out of the pennant race after May. If there had been a chance of a title, the fans would have been there.

As for homer 711, it made Hank think again about the record. "I have a shot," he said. "This one enhances the chances. We've got 10 games left and I'm going to try to play in as many as I can."

One of the visitors in the Atlanta locker room after

the game was Commissioner Kuhn, who had patched up his earlier differences with Hank. Kuhn spotted Hank surrounded by reporters and teased:

"You're quite a show-off!"

Then the Commissioner had an announcement of his own.

"I'm extremely pleased to tell you that Hank Aaron will throw out the first ball of the 1973 world series. This is the first time to my knowledge that an active player has been given this honor. But it is baseball's way of showing Hank just how much he has meant to all of us."

And one reporter covering the game chose to ignore the obvious.

"All the attention has been on Hank's homers," he wrote, "and rightly so. But in case you failed to notice, the man is now batting a crisp .290. He's been around .350 since the all-star break and I don't think anyone in baseball has hit any better. At 39, he still swings a better bat for my money than anyone in the game."

Five more days passed. Then on September 22, Hank whipped his strong wrists around and tied into a Dave Roberts fastball. Number 712 sailed into the far reaches of Houston's large Astrodome. It was an interesting game for several reasons.

First of all, Roberts was one of the pitchers who had said he was determined to stop Hank. ("I'm glad it wasn't the 714th or 715th," he said later.) And, secondly, it was the Braves' final road game. They had five left, three with the Dodgers and two more with the Astros, all at the launching pad in Atlanta.

"I just want to hurry and get it over with," was Hank's comment. "I can't recall a day at the end of last year or all this year when I didn't hear the name of Babe Ruth. It gets a little wearing. But one thing's for sure. As much as I want to end it, I'm still not going up there and pressing for homers. Right now, I'd say my chances for doing it this year aren't too good. The bat is getting kind of heavy this time of year. I dropped down to a 33 against Roberts, and I may wind up things in Atlanta with a 32."

So it came down to five games. The crowds picked up for the set with L.A., perhaps 10,000 for one game, 5,000 for another. Then Hank lost a big opportunity when the third was rained out and couldn't be rescheduled. He got no homers.

"You can't do anything about the weather," he lamented. "That brings it down to two with Houston."

Lefthander Jerry Reuss started the first game for the Astros. Batting in the cleanup position, Hank singled in the first inning as the Braves scored two runs. He walked in the third, then came up again in the fifth. This time there were two men on.

Reuss tried some finesse stuff first, then came back with the fastball. The timing and the wrists were still there. Hank jerked the pitch to deep left. It went out! Number 713! And the crowd of 17,836 fans screamed wildly as their hero circled the bases. He was making it interesting, all right.

Hank got one chance to tie it in this game. He came up again in the eighth against righty reliever Larry Dierker. Dierker was one of the pitchers who had been reprimanded by Kuhn earlier in the year for saying he'd groove one if the time was right. Maybe Henry remembered that. Anyway, he worked the count full, three and two. Dierker delivered and Hank went after it, but the result was just a bloop hit to left.

"I hadn't pitched in three weeks," Dierker said, after the game. "But I was really keyed up out there, knowing he had a chance to tie the record. It was really exciting. But the situation was different than I thought it would be. I worked on him. Who knows, if I'm in there tomorrow and we're ahead, 10-1, then I might challenge him with a fastball."

So it came down to one last game in '73. The Houston starter was none other than Dave Roberts, who had given up number 712 to Hank a week earlier; he was a confirmed Aaron stopper if the chance was there.

"If he comes up with a chance to beat me with a home run, I'm gonna pitch around him," Roberts said, flatly.

Hank came up for the first time in the opening inning. The count went 1-1 and then he topped one to third. Hustling down the line, he beat it out for a base hit. In the fourth, he faced the lefty again. The count was again even at 1-1 when Hank connected for a solid single to center. In the sixth, Roberts had two strikes on Hank when he singled up the middle again.

The lefty's back stiffened in the seventh and righty Don Wilson was on the mound when Hank came to bat in the eighth. Wilson had reportedly told a cabdriver that he'd give Hank something good if he got the chance. But his first pitch was on the hands and Hank went after it, lofting a harmless pop to the infield. Just like that it was over.

"Yeah, this time I was going for the long one," Hank admitted. "I didn't want base hits. But Roberts gave me only one good pitch all afternoon."

The Houston hurler confirmed this. "The first pitch I threw him was the only good one. I tried to keep the ball away from him. If he was going to get one, he'd have to get it off one of those. There was pressure and I didn't get him out, but at least I kept it in the park. The man may be 39, but he's got 19-year-old wrists."

Some people criticized Manager Mathews for not batting Hank leadoff, which would have given him an extra at-bat.

"I didn't want that," Hank said. "I might have if it was my last season."

So he came up one short. But just take a look at the kind of season this 39-year-old wonderman had.

Henry played in 120 games. He had 118 hits in 392

at-bats, including six hits in his last seven trips to give him a final batting average of .301. And not even Henry thought he'd hit .300 again. Among his hits were 12 doubles, one triple, and 40 big home runs. Amazing. And he batted in 96 runs, missing the 100 mark by just four. In addition, the old man led the entire Braves team in game-winning RBI's with 12. It had to be one of the most amazing seasons ever put together, especially under the conditions Henry experienced.

After Henry showered and dressed there was a final, official press conference. One writer described how Henry appeared as he took his seat, center stage.

"He settled into his seat and a warm genuine smile came to his face. There was no sign of tension from the attention he had been subjected to since people began realizing he was going to break one of the most cherished records of all sports. He had shaken the Establishment to the roots."

Hank was patient and receptive to the reporters' questions. He admitted he was disappointed that he didn't get the record, maybe because he knew he'd be facing the same questions all over again in '74. He thanked the 40,000 some-odd fans who had come out the final day, and called the long, standing ovation he received after his final at bat "the greatest thing that ever happened to me."

He said the tension began bothering him the final month, but added, "I've got another year and I'm going to spend the winter resting up. But I can't hide. I've got to live my life."

The life is in very sharp focus now. Though he had never been asked to do many commercials before, Hank signed a contract with the famous William Morris Agency, and a spokesman claimed that he'd earn between $1.5 million and $2 million during the coming two years. And this would be aside from his baseball income.

There were tentative plans for an autobiography and a possible movie about his life. Also trips abroad and many more endorsements and commercials.

"I've waited very patiently for this," Hank said. "By comparison to other players, I've made very little in outside income. I just kept the faith and played the game as it's supposed to be played."

Though Hank's first marriage ended in divorce several years ago, he still spends a great deal of time with his four children. He has also remarried, and his wife is a personality in her own right, hosting a daily television talk show in Atlanta.

So there's no reason to believe that Hank won't relax and enjoy what will likely be his final year as an active player. And with his ability, he'll probably turn in another fine season.

Then what? Hank has indicated that he'd like to stay in baseball. Managing isn't for him, he's said, but he might like to try his hand at being a general manager.

"I want to play an active role," he's said, "not just take up space in a figurehead position."

Whatever he does, one thing is for certain. Henry Aaron will do it well. The 1973 season only served to reiterate that Mr. Aaron is a very remarkable athlete and a very remarkable man as well.

Some years ago, Hank was asked how he'd like to be remembered. Without hesitating, he replied, "I don't want to be anything special or anyone special. I just want to be remembered as plain Henry Aaron."

Well, for once in his life, he was wrong. There's no way that he'll be remembered as plain Henry Aaron. No matter how you cut the pie, Henry Louis Aaron is special. He is very special indeed.

Hank Aaron

Statistics

Year	Club	G	AB	R	H	2B	3B	HR	RBI	BA
1952	Eau Claire	87	345	79	116	19	4	9	61	.336
1953	Jacksonville	137	574	115	208	36	14	22	125	.362
1954	Milwaukee	122	468	58	131	27	6	13	69	.280
1955	Milwaukee	153	602	105	189	37	9	27	106	.314
1956	Milwaukee	153	609	106	200	34	14	26	92	.328
1957	Milwaukee	151	615	118	198	27	6	44	132	.322
1958	Milwaukee	153	601	109	196	34	4	30	95	.326
1959	Milwaukee	154	629	116	223	46	7	39	123	.355
1960	Milwaukee	153	590	102	172	20	11	40	126	.292
1961	Milwaukee	155	603	115	197	39	10	34	120	.327
1962	Milwaukee	156	592	127	191	28	6	45	128	.323
1963	Milwaukee	161	631	121	201	29	4	44	130	.319
1964	Milwaukee	145	570	103	187	30	2	24	95	.328
1965	Milwaukee	150	570	109	181	40	1	32	89	.318
1966	Atlanta	158	603	117	168	23	1	44	127	.279
1967	Atlanta	155	600	113	184	37	3	39	109	.307
1968	Atlanta	160	606	84	174	33	4	29	86	.287
1969	Atlanta	147	547	100	164	30	3	44	97	.300
1970	Atlanta	150	516	103	154	26	1	38	118	.298
1971	Atlanta	139	495	95	162	22	3	47	118	.327
1972	Atlanta	129	449	75	119	10	0	34	77	.265
1973	Atlanta	120	392	84	118	12	1	40	96	.310
Major League Totals		2964	11288	2060	3509	584	96	713	2133	.311

Bobby Murcer

BILL GUTMAN

Revised and updated from AT BAT

GROSSET & DUNLAP
Publishers   New York

For Beth

A Tempo Double Book
Tempo Books is registered in the U.S. Patent Office

Published simultaneously in Canada
Printed in the United States of America

ACKNOWLEDGMENTS

The author wishes to thank the following people for their help in supplying background material for this book: Marty Appel, of the New York Yankees, as well as the publicity department of the team; Kevin Fitzgerald at *Sport* Magazine; Brooks Moser, of Southeast High School; and Mr. and Mrs. Robert Murcer, Ralph Houk, and Tom Greenwade.

Bobby Murcer

Bobby Murcer

BEING A YANKEE has never been easy for Bobby Murcer. The reason is totally unrelated to Bobby's talents as a ballplayer. It has to do with tradition, New York Yankee tradition, and the quirk of fate that put Bobby Murcer in pinstripes at a particular point in Yankee history.

Bobby came to the Yanks for good in 1969. Coincidentally, that was also the first year in the past 49 that the Bomber attack was missing one of its most treasured trademarks. There was no reigning superstar. And the word superstar had been synonymous with the Yankees ever since the immortal Babe Ruth first donned the New York colors in 1920.

Then in 1925, the Babe was joined by Lou Gehrig, and the two sluggers made their own special mayhem

1

until the Babe left in 1934. Gehrig continued to bust fences until stopped by illness in 1939. By that time, a youngster named Joe DiMaggio was already in his fourth year with the club and was fast becoming the next great superplayer.

DiMag led the Yankee dynasty through the 1951 season, when he announced his retirement. And with typical Yankee magic, that was the same year the team came up with a rookie named Mickey Mantle. The bloodline continued with the famed Switcher until 1968, when Mickey decided his battered legs could take the pounding no longer. He went to spring training in 1969, but then abruptly quit.

Suddenly, there was a look of desperation in the eyes of Yankee rooters. Ruth . . . Gehrig . . . DiMaggio . . . Mantle. They had followed each other in such a neat, orderly fashion that most people thought it was preordained. Shouldn't the next Yankee superslugger have been signed, sealed and delivered when Mickey was ready to call it a career?

But where was he? Maybe it was Joe Pepitone, or Tom Tresh. But they had been around a few years already and were settling into the comfortable position of ballplayers who never reached their original potential. They just weren't superstars. The eyes continued to search.

Then someone spotted a youngster in camp, looked at the roster, and found the name Bobby Murcer. A check of the records revealed some interesting facts. Murcer was from Oklahoma, just like Mickey. And he

had been signed by Tom Greenwade, the same scout who inked Mantle. This had to be the guy, the next great Yankee superstar.

The word was out. The papers picked it up, the fans jumped on the bandwagon, and people talked about it wherever Bobby went. Right away, the youngster would be playing in shadows. There were shoes to be filled, big shoes, traditional shoes, shoes that had been worn proudly for half a century. It was a huge burden for any person to bear.

Bobby had been up with the Yanks before, in 1965 and 1966. He had brief trials each time and hadn't been able to put together his hitting and fielding. He was expected to stick in '67 when he received his greetings from Uncle Sam. So the army cost him another two years. By 1969, he was back and ready.

Only the timing was bad. Mantle had just retired and Yankee fans were anxious for another hero. They wanted one right away. And for a while, Bobby seemed to be their man.

Though not a massive slugger in the traditional sense, the 5-11, 180-pound Murcer had a sweet stroke from the left side of the plate. He choked up on the bat slightly, yet the ball jumped when he connected. During spring training, he sprayed sharp line drives all over the lot. He seemed calm and collected. Nothing bothered him. Murcer looked like a hitter all the way.

When the reporters started coming around, their questions were obvious. How did Bobby feel about

3

being touted as the new Yankee superstar, the successor to Mantle, and the reincarnation of the spirit personified by Ruth, Gehrig and DiMaggio?

It was a poised Murcer who answered them with a self-assurance that belied his 22 years.

"Sure, it's nice to dream about being a superstar," he said. "Any ballplayer would like being one and getting all the things that go with it . . . the television, the opportunities to make some money, and the interesting people you'd meet. But let's face it, even if I'm good enough to be called a superstar some day, I'm not going to do it in one year.

"In fact, I'm not a leader now and I'm certainly not a star. Mickey was the leader here and he's gone. But there are other guys who have been around awhile and have contributed to the success of the club. Heck, just five years ago I was watching all of them on television."

Bobby handled himself so well that he was a popular figure with the media people immediately. But they just wouldn't let go with the superstar bit. Everyone was waiting for the start of the regular season to see if the new Oklahoma kid was the real thing.

They found out in a hurry. The season opened for the Yanks at Washington. In the third inning of that first game, another Bomber rookie cracked a home run over the rightfield fence. Then Murcer stepped in.

Bobby studied the pitcher from his slightly closed stance, midway in the lefthand batters' box. He wag-

4

gled his bat a few times, then got set. The Washington hurler threw a fastball and Bobby snapped those quick wrists. CRACK! He could feel the good wood from his hands up to his shoulders. And when he looked up, he saw the ball soaring high and deep to rightfield.

He took off toward first, and as he rounded the bag, the ball settled deep in the upper deck. He couldn't believe he had hit it so far. It was a great feeling, and the fans in New York thanked their television sets for allowing them to witness the birth of the next Yankee superstar.

Once again, Bobby had to deal with waves of reporters after the game. It didn't faze him. The next day he went out and belted another one, this time a line shot that rocketed into the lower stands. At the end of the first week, rookie Murcer was batting .393 and the Yanks were heading home. Stadium stalwarts couldn't wait to see their newest hero in person.

And what a debut he made! In the first game he quickly stroked homer number three into the short porch in rightfield. That done, he proceeded to rip a hard double down the line in right. A single to center was his third hit of the afternoon. He had driven home four runs. The youngster from Oklahoma City just couldn't be stopped.

The next day he proved it wasn't a fluke by belting another homer. And the day after that he did it again. Murcer had cracked five homers in the Yanks' first nine games!

Yankee fans wasted no time in discovering Bobby Murcer. They began to flock to the ballpark as soon as the word was out, and Bobby drew more cheers than any of the veteran players on the team. When someone asked Yankee president Michael Burke if the team was out to create another superstar, Burke answered:

"I don't think you can create a superstar. It's just there in the man himself and all you can do is hope that it comes out. The fact that Bobby's hitting the ball the way he is is just there. We have all seen it together. We don't have to promote anything. The newspapers and television cameras took care of it for us. Now the fans know about it and they want to jump on the bandwagon. They all want to get out and see Bobby now. Then, if he makes it big, they can say they were here when he was just breaking in."

No matter how you looked at it, Bobby was the talk of the town. When the season was just six weeks old, Bobby Murcer was still hitting .324, the fifth best mark in the American League. He had already belted 10 home runs and his runs-batted-in total of 38 was better than anyone else in the major leagues. Everyone was singing the praises of the rookie.

But baseball has always been known as a game of inches. And to some more astute observers, Murcer was beginning to lose the edge. For one thing, he was having a frustrating time of it in the field. Bobby had come to the Yanks as a shortstop in 1956. Now, the Bombers were trying him at third base. It wasn't easy.

6

In those early games which saw him hit the homers and drive in all the runs, Bobby had made 14 errors at the hot corner.

"Bobby was just too erratic with his hands and arm," said Yank manager Ralph Houk. "What it amounted to was that he didn't really know what to do out there."

Then toward the end of May, Bobby injured a heel and missed several games. When he returned, his Midas touch was gone. So was the sweet stroke that terrorized American League pitchers for six weeks. "I don't know how it happened," Bobby said. "But it seemed that my timing just disappeared."

The rest of the season became a struggle for young Bobby Murcer and the rest of the Yanks. All the high hopes of the spring dissolved into the humidity of the long summer, and the eyes of Stadium fans began to shift out to the borough of Queens, where the other New York team, the Mets, was making some music of its own. Before 1969 ended, all of New York had jumped on the Met bandwagon. The perennial league doormats were en route to an amazing pennant and World Series triumph. Most people forgot there was even a New York Yankee team. And Bobby Murcer, well, he was just a flash in the pan anyway.

How, then, did this well-mannered young man from Oklahoma work his way into the unenviable position of being looked upon as the new Ruth-Gehrig-DiMaggio-Mantle? Blame it on history. It just put him in a

certain place at a certain time and told him to produce.

Bobby Ray Murcer was born on May 20, 1946, at St. Anthony Hospital in Oklahoma City, Oklahoma. His parents, Robert and Maybelle Murcer, had two other sons. Dwayne, the eldest, is five years Bobby's senior, while Randy is seven years younger than Bobby.

Unlike the fathers of most top athletes, Bobby's dad wasn't a ballplayer, and he often said of his son: "I'm not sure where he got his ability, but he must have been born with it inside him. He was athletic from the time he was two years old and he always had a ball in his hands from that time on. I used to play catch with him very often and he'd ask me to throw grounders at him, then pop-ups. He loved it, even then."

Bobby's mother describes him as "an ornery kid who ran away from home three or four times when he was young. But he never got very far and used to come back and apologize. I guess he had a bit of a temper even then, but basically, he was a very good boy."

When he reached the age of six or seven, Bobby was playing in the Pee Wee League. He participated in all the sports then, but was already becoming interested in baseball, as were many Oklahoma boys in those days. It was the time when Mickey Mantle was just beginning to make his presence felt with the Yankees, and the boys back home followed their hero's exploits with awe and adulation.

But before long, Bobby was just as active in football and basketball as he was with baseball. They took up all his time.

"So many of the young boys did other things," said Mrs. Murcer, "like play Cowboys and Indians, or fool around with their toy guns. Not Bobby. It was just sports and more sports with him ever since I can remember."

Brooks Moser remembers Bobby, too. Moser was the football and baseball coach at Southeast High School in Oklahoma City. But he met Bobby even before that, when the youngster was one of his students in his eighth grade history class.

"Bobby was a real little guy then," Moser recalls. "He must have weighed all of sixty pounds. I wouldn't have thought that in just two years he would become one of the best all-around athletes I ever coached. But I soon found out that the kid had a heart as big as a watermelon. He was a winner all the way. He thinks win, and that's the most important thing."

The Murcers were also concerned about Bobby's size. After all, he played rough and tumble all day long and most of the other boys were bigger than he was.

"Of course I worried," said Mrs. Murcer. "All mothers do. I didn't think he was big enough, especially for football. But I'll say one thing. Bobby never worried about his size. He didn't let it bother him one bit. And believe it or not, as reckless as he was when he

played, he never once got hurt seriously all through high school."

Then Mr. Murcer added, "Sometimes Bobby talked about lifting weights. I really didn't approve of it, except for building up the legs, so he stuck to that. He was aware of being small then, but he always said if Phil Rizzuto could make it as a fast little man, he could too. Even then, he wanted to be the shortstop of the Yankees."

Bobby got tired of baseball once in his life. It happened when he was about 12 or 13. "He just came up to me one night and said he was sick of baseball and he wasn't going to play any more," Mr. Murcer said. "I guess one of the other sports was in season then, because his feeling didn't last long. As soon as it was time again, he grabbed his glove and got back out there."

By the time Bobby reached Southeast High, he was a little bigger, around 5-7, 110 pounds. He never weighed more than 145 at Southwest, so he'll always be remembered as a little guy, even now.

"Pound for pound, Bobby Murcer was the best high school ballplayer I ever coached," said Brooks Moser. "He was tough as a boot, and you can't teach toughness. I remember that he started as a sophomore on the football team and weighed 110 pounds. I knew he had desire and ability, but I wondered about his size. Pretty soon he was challenging guys 40-50 pounds heavier than he was. It didn't bother him a bit.

"Bobby was a running back on offense and a line-

backer on defense. By the time he was a senior in 1964, he weighed 145 pounds and he was the hardest running 145-pounder I've ever seen. He was a smart player, too. He always knew what he was doing out there."

On the baseball diamond, Moser was just as impressed with the youngster's skills.

"He started playing for me when he was just a soph," the coach recalls. "He had great ability even then. And he had the best batting eye I've ever seen. He was amazing with the bat; he always made contact. In his senior year he struck out just three times and hit about .350.

"He was also a great leader in high school. He always helped the younger boys and gave them his time. Being a star never went to his head. He led by ability and the other boys respected him. He wasn't a power hitter then, but he hit sharp line drives, and got a lot of singles and doubles. He played shortstop for me and did a nice job, although his arm was somewhat erratic."

Bobby was an all-state gridiron and diamond performer for Southeast High, and even found time to make the all-city basketball team. He was a quick guard and averaged close to 20 points a game, though he never loved the court game as much as baseball and football.

In his senior year, he had two outstanding games, one in football, one in baseball, that will always stand out in the mind of Brooks Moser.

"Our football team was playing Harding High for the conference title in 1965. We had a 6-0 lead, and it was late in the game. Harding drove downfield on us and got a first down on the four-yard line. I really didn't think we could hold them.

"On four straight plays, they ran the ball off-tackle. And each time the man who made the initial contact and stopped the play was our middle linebacker, 145-pound Bobby Murcer. He was unbelievable. He must have been really fired up. He just picked the play, filled the hole and stuck the ballcarrier. I always called it a one-man goal-line stand. He really made it possible for us to win that one.

"Then during the baseball season, we had a similar key game against Ulysses S. Grant High, another arch-rival. All Bobby did that day was get four hits, including a real clout in the sixth inning that he legged out for a home run. And that's the one that won the game for us. It seems he was always coming through in the pinch."

By this time, Bobby was thinking about other things, namely his future. He was a good student with a B-average. Several colleges were already making him scholarship offers because of his athletic ability. But the baseball scouts were coming around, too.

"Baseball was always Bobby's first love," said Brooks Moser. "He always wanted to be a big leaguer. But he really liked the contact and competition in football, too. I think he just realized that baseball offered him a better opportunity for a career.

"Bobby signed a letter of intent to attend Oklahoma University when he was a senior with me. They wanted him as a football player and were thinking of making him a wide receiver. When he asked me what I thought he should do, I told him to go ahead and play baseball if he really wanted to. If he went to college, he might lose his bonus. But if things didn't go well, he could always return to school."

It was a difficult decision that many young men are forced to make. And it's hard to say what the right choice is. Bobby had grown some, but he was still very small for big time football and that might have influenced his decision. Then there was still his old dream.

"Mickey Mantle had been my idol for a long time," he said. "And it was always in the back of my mind to play with the Yankees someday, maybe even on the same team with him. I guess that had something to do with my decision. If the Yankees didn't show an interest, I really don't know what would have happened."

Mrs. Murcer remembers those days well. "Scouts were calling us as early as Bobby's junior year in high school," she said. "I remember the night he graduated, there were five or six scouts waiting by the door. But Bobby always had his mind set on the Yanks. It was his dream ever since he was a small boy."

Even when the scouts came around, fate was already taking a hand, preparing Bobby for his eventual

destiny with the Yanks. The scout who was in charge of the Oklahoma territory for the New York club was Tom Greenwade, the very same man who signed another Oklahoman some 15 years earlier. That youngster's name was Mickey Mantle.

"There's no way I can honestly compare Bobby and Mickey," Tom Greenwade says. "They were different types of ballplayers. Mickey was a switch hitter and Bobby's strictly a lefty. I don't think Bobby ran as well as young Mickey did. And, of course, Mickey was a lot bigger and stronger than Bobby."

Tom Greenwade knows baseball talent as well as anyone. He's been in baseball for some 50 years and with the Yanks for more than 30. Working from his home base in Willard, Missouri, Greenwade roams all over several states looking for young prospects. Though the scouting system has changed somewhat in recent years, there are many similarities from the old days.

"A scout is in charge of a specific territory," explains Greenwade. "And it's up to him to organize that territory. He has to recruit a number of 'bird dogs' or sub scouts who can spot potential talent for him. They can be almost anyone from high school coaches to local businessmen who love sports.

"And the scout himself must be acquainted with coaches and fans. If people know and like you, they'll tip you off to a good kid. And you've got to check every tip, even though sometimes you take one look and know it won't work out.

"These days, scouts generally make regular reports to the parent club. It's necessary under the free agent system so they can be ready to draft. But in the old days, the scout simply knew the openings on the team and worked accordingly. Believe it or not, the Yankees never even knew about Mantle until I had the signed contract with him.

"So it's really up to the scout to make the signing decision. Maybe not with some of the younger guys, but it's always been that way with me. The only time I go to the club for advice is if the boy is asking for too much money, or more than I'm authorized to offer."

Of course, there are specific qualities that scouts look for in young ballplayers and Tom Greenwade has his own particular way of doing it. It's the system he used when he began looking at Bobby Murcer.

"The first thing I look at is a boy's throwing arm," he said. "I worked for Branch Rickey once and he always said that baseball was a throwing game. A boy with a good arm can play somewhere. Then I look for speed. If he can throw and run, that's two of the three qualities. Hitting, naturally, is the third. After that comes the intangibles like temperament and attitude.

"I can tell a 'live' arm very quickly. Then I have to consider the boy's age. Will the arm get better? If a boy can throw and has a good body, then perhaps you can overlook light hitting. Many youngsters chase curveballs and swing at bad pitches. I remember both

15

Pepper Martin and Pee Wee Reese were two guys who couldn't touch a curve when they first came up. But they learned, and before they were through, both were known as good curveball hitters. If, by chance, you find a boy who can hit and pull the ball at the same time, then you've got yourself an exception."

But there's no foolproof method of tabbing a future big league star, and Tom Greenwade doesn't care for the words "can't miss," which are used so often in describing the current season's hot prospects.

"When you sign a kid out of high school, you don't think about whether he'll make it big or not. You simply say to yourself, here's a kid who has a chance. Some make it, some don't. You've got to have reservations because so many things can happen. So much of it depends on a youngster's attitude and determination, plus the tools he has to begin with. I've signed some boys who should have made it, but didn't.

"Then there's the other side of the coin," the old scout continued. "I never realized that Mantle would be so outstanding when I signed him, not until that first season with the Yanks. The same thing happened when I signed George Kell. Then there were boys who I was even higher on and they didn't make it. That's why I never say a kid can't miss."

Tom Greenwade saw Bobby Murcer for the first time in August of 1963. Bobby was playing American Legion ball that summer, waiting for his senior year in high school to begin.

"One of my bird dogs, an insurance man named

Howard Parkey, had been watching Bobby for some time. He finally was convinced that Bobby had the makings and asked me to come down and take a look. I told him that we had another scout in the area and I'd get in touch with him.

"Well, this other guy goes down there with Parkey and he's not too high on Bobby. He thought Bobby bailed out against lefthanders and had a bad temper. Parkey contacted the guy again and told him that a lot of other scouts were beginning to look at the kid. But this guy said he wasn't interested. So when Parkey told me about the situation, I jumped on a train and got right on down there. I respected Parkey's judgment.

"I was impressed immediately. Bobby was obviously a good hitter. He made contact and I didn't see any real problems against lefties. He played short and had the good, live arm. But he also had what we call 'hard hands,' but that's something we can overlook at the early stage. If he continued to play the infield, I think he might have overcome it.

"He also had a world of confidence in himself. I liked that. But he did have a bad temper, especially on the football field. I was told, and when I talked to him I advised him to get better control of himself.

"Anyway, I knew that the Red Sox and Dodgers were also interested in him at the time, so I told him not to forget the Yanks and that I wanted to take him to Kansas City for a tryout after he graduated in June."

Bobby then settled into playing all three sports at Southeast during his senior year of 1963-64. Meanwhile, Tom Greenwade was in touch with the Murcer family.

"I think Bobby's dad favored football," he said. "I know Bobby was thinking about baseball then and indicated he was considering sitting out the football season. But his dad wanted him to play and he did. It's lucky he wasn't hurt seriously."

True to his word, Tom Greenwade took Bobby up to Kansas City immediately after he graduated. The Yanks ran a tryout camp there and many of the club officials came down to take a look at the prospects.

Ralph Houk was the Yanks' general manager that year, and he approached Tom Greenwade after the workout.

"What are you going to do about the Murcer kid?" Houk asked.

"I'm gonna sign him," was Greenwade's answer.

Houk smiled. "I hope you do."

After some brief negotiations with Bobby and his family, everything was set. In June of 1964, Bobby Murcer became the property of the New York Yankees. He received a modest bonus, and shunned a rival offer that would have paid him about $1,000 more. He wanted to be a Yankee, though at the time he didn't realize the problems that went along with it. The Yanks immediately assigned the youngster to Johnson City, Tennessee, to play for their farm team in the Appalachian League.

"We were a little worried about Bobby's going so far away," said Mrs. Murcer. "He had to fly down there and he had never even stepped on a plane before."

But off he went, an 18-year-old shortstop on his way to Johnson City for his first glimpse of life as a professional ballplayer. He had grown since those early days and now stood about 5-10 and was gaining weight. He was almost up to 160 pounds, so he was no longer the little guy. But when he arrived at Johnson City, he found there were some strange things expected of minor leaguers.

"When I got there, I found out that the first thing we had to do was put the field in shape," Bobby said. "In other words, the players were the groundskeepers. We had to pick up rocks and litter, and smooth the whole thing out. I was beginning to wonder if pro ball was everything it was cracked up to be."

But once that was done, Bobby settled down to the business of playing ball. He played in 32 games and was peppering line drives all over the lot. Hitting Appalachian League pitching was no trouble for him. He smacked out 46 safeties in 126 at-bats for a .365 average. He only hit two homers, but he drove in 29 runs. His season was cut short by a knee injury.

"I got banged up sliding into home during the first game of a doubleheader," he recalled. "It's funny, but I didn't even know it at the time. I was sitting out the second game anyway and just relaxed in the dugout.

But when the game was over, my knee was twice its size and I could hardly walk on it."

The Yanks didn't want to take any chances with Murcer. They immediately made arrangements for Bobby to come to New York to be examined by the team physician, Dr. Sidney Gaynor.

"I was pretty excited about it," he confessed. "It was my first trip ever to New York, even if it was because of an injury. The only hitch was that my flight landed in Newark, and that really threw me for a loop. I didn't even know how to get to New York from there. Somehow I made it to Dr. Gaynor's office. He found that a sac under my kneecap had burst and there was fluid all over the place. It had to be drained a couple of times, but it wasn't serious.

"The funny part was that I was only in New York for a day. The Yankees were on the road, so I didn't meet any of them. And I didn't even have a chance to go out and see the Stadium. The next thing I knew I was back in Johnson City."

But the Yanks didn't leave Bobby in Johnson City for long. He hit too well for that. The next year they sent him to Greensboro in the Carolina League. That's where he started turning on the power. Playing in 126 games, he had 16 home runs among his 154 hits, and he drove in 90 runs. His batting average was a healthy .322, and the word was that his fielding was getting better. When the Carolina League season ended, the Yanks called him up for the final weeks of the 1965 major league campaign.

Bobby had come in at the tail end of the parade, although he didn't realize it at the time. The New Yorkers had taken their fifth straight pennant in 1964, and their ninth in ten years. Even though they were beaten in the World Series by the Cards that year, it seemed as if the dynasty would continue. There was a blend of old and young players with absolutely no indication that the team was about to decline.

A young ballplayer like Bobby, signed by the Yanks in 1964, could only feel that he was going to the best team in all of baseball and would have a difficult time cracking the starting lineup. How was Bobby or anyone else to know that in the next few years the following things would happen to the team:

Mickey Mantle's great skills would diminish quickly and irreversibly; Roger Maris would be traded; Tom Tresh and Joe Pepitone would fail to live up to superslugger billing; Clete Boyer would be dealt away; Tony Kubek and Bobby Richardson would both retire prematurely.

No, it was impossible to foresee any of that. But in the 1965 season, the seemingly invincible Yankees suddenly nosedived to a 77-85 record and a sixth-place finish. That's the kind of situation Bobby entered when he was brought up for a "look."

Bobby didn't see too much action with the Yanks. He got into 11 games at shortstop, was unsure of himself in the field, but showed a good batting stroke. He was zero for the first seven at-bats when he came up against righthander Jim Duckworth of Washington.

Duckworth thought he'd fool the youngster with a curve, but Bobby timed it perfectly and sent a screaming liner out toward rightfield. It just kept carrying and finally settled into the lower stands. Bobby couldn't believe it. His first big league hit had been a home run. It seemed all the more unbelievable when one of the players shaking his hand back in the dugout was Mickey Mantle. It was his old dream come true at last.

But that was the only homer he hit. He finished with a .243 average, and four runs batted in. And neither he nor the Yanks had an idea of what awaited the team in 1966. After all, the New York Yankees had been baseball's dominant ballclub since 1920. And when they occasionally fell from the pedestal, they always got up and climbed the mountain again fast.

Not this time. Something wasn't right. The players didn't seem to have the old zip. Then shortstop Tony Kubek was forced into retirement because of a neck injury. Without warning, 19-year-old Bobby Murcer found himself in the running for the starting shortstop position. It was the first of many pressures he was going to feel in the next several seasons.

He started the spring very well. Once again he had the good batting stroke and was meeting the ball solidly. Older players, fans and newsmen said the same thing, "The kid looks like a hitter." He still wasn't sure of himself in the field, but he was getting by, and he figured he'd improve.

Midway through the training season, Yank manager Johnny Keane, who had managed the Cards to a World Series win over the New Yorkers in 1964, told the press that Murcer would get the first crack at the starting shortstop job. In other words, all Bobby had to do was keep things on an even keel and he was the Yankee shortstop.

"Wow," Murcer says now, "that's when I really started to think about it. Maybe before that I didn't realize how close I was to playing major league baseball with the Yankees. I guess I wasn't ready, because when Keane said that I'd likely be the starting shortstop, I was really overawed.

"I suddenly found myself thinking about being alongside all those great players. I really thought the team would bounce back. The thought of my teammates and a pennant race ... the whole thing overwhelmed me."

And it came out in Bobby's weakest suit—fielding. Suddenly, he couldn't hold onto anything and he couldn't throw straight. The errors came in bunches and manager Keane began to have second thoughts. When Bobby's hitting began to fade, too, Keane made his decision. Veteran journeyman Ruben Amaro would have to play short until Murcer, or someone else, was ready.

"That was a real crusher to me," Bobby said. "I felt like crying when I made all those errors. I knew that I had blown my chance."

So the 1966 season opened with Amaro at short and

23

Murcer on the bench. Amaro played five games for the Yanks. Then there was a collision at second base and the veteran was carried from the field with a severe knee injury. The next day, Bobby Murcer was at shortstop.

The game, played at Baltimore, was a disaster for Bobby. He made three key errors and the Yanks bowed, 5-4. The next day, third baseman Clete Boyer was at short and Bobby was back on the bench. In the following two weeks, Keane used him only as a pinch runner. Then, with the Yankee record at a dismal 4-16, and morale at an all-time low, Keane was fired. And a byproduct of the move that returned Ralph Houk to the field manager's spot, was the demotion of Bobby Murcer to Toledo of the International League. The kid needed more seasoning, they said.

It wasn't easy for Bobby to face another year in the minors, especially in the wake of the great expectations of just a few weeks before. Here he was with the chance of a lifetime, to become the regular shortstop on the New York Yankees. He wasn't yet 20 years old, and Bobby himself blamed his collapse on not being ready, in other words, on immaturity.

Once at Toledo, Bobby settled down. There wasn't the pressure at the minor league club and he relaxed to play his own game. But by midseason, he hit a dry spell and it taught him something.

"Slumps used to really get me," Bobby said. "I'd get down and get depressed. But at Toledo, I learned not

to worry about slumps. I was going real good and suddenly I had a spell where I got just three hits in 60 at-bats. After that, I figured I'd never have one as bad as that again. So why worry."

Even with the slump, Bobby finished the 1966 season at Toledo with a .266 batting average. He had 15 homers and 62 RBI's. He showed his usual sharp work with the bat. Fielding was something Bobby still had to work on, and he worried about it. But he looked forward to another good shot with the Yanks in '67.

The reason he knew he'd have a chance was simple. The Bronx Bombers had hit rock bottom. When Bobby came up again at the end of the season, he found a worn-out, disintegrating team. The Yanks were in 10th place, dead last, just two years after taking the American League pennant. Manager Houk used the rookie in about 20 games at the tail end of the year. Bobby batted a disappointing .174 with just 12 hits in 69 at-bats. The team finished with a 70-89 mark and faced a major rebuilding job.

So Bobby returned to Oklahoma, more confident than he had ever been before. Last spring he had been awed by the legendary Yankee stars. Now he'd be trying out for a last-place club. Psychologically, he was in a better frame of mind. He was sure he would make the team in 1967.

That October, Bobby married Kay Rhodes of Oklahoma City, a girl he'd been dating since he was 15 years old. The two of them left for Fort Lauderdale, Florida, the following February. Kay was expecting

their first child, and Bobby was confident he'd be with the Yanks for good.

Before he left Oklahoma, Bobby had applied for acceptance into an army reserve unit. He figured there would be little problem and he could work out his schedule as soon as he found which unit he was in. He got a letter, all right, but it wasn't from a reserve unit. It was from the draft board itself. Bobby Murcer had been drafted into the regular Army.

The news was a shock to Bobby, and to the Yanks. Houk and his staff were anxious to take a long look at the kid. Now they'd have to wait two years. It was a bitter disappointment. Bobby and Kay packed again and returned home. He said goodbye and left for basic training at Fort Bliss, Texas.

After Basic, Bobby was assigned to Fort Huachua, Arizona, where he remained for the entire two years. He was with a radio unit and really didn't have to work very hard. But he missed baseball. He hated to lose the two years.

"I really wanted to play some kind of ball while I was there," Bobby said. "But the only way I could play would be to make a 140-mile round trip. And that would be to play a little semi-pro stuff. It just wasn't worth it.

"The only good thing about my army job was that my wife could join me, and our daughter Tori was born right on the army post so I could be close by. I guess that makes her an army brat. She won't believe

it when I take her back there some day and show her where she was born."

But time passes, and when Bobby got his release early in 1969, it was almost spring training time again. The Yanks had made some improvement while he was gone. In '67, they were 72-90 and in ninth place. The next year, 1968, the team rebounded to an 83-79 mark and climbed all the way to fifth. But while there were certain plusses that year, there was a major minus, also.

The 1968 season served notice that the end was very near for Mickey Mantle. The one-time superslugger batted a hobbling .237, with 18 homers and 54 RBI's. He was a shell of his former self, struck out too much and played with pain in his battered legs. If Mickey quit, it would signal perhaps the end of another Yankee tradition, the presence of a super ballplayer.

Mantle did quit early in the spring of 1969. And almost immediately, added pressure fell on to the shoulders of young Bobby Murcer.

The first time Bobby took batting practice that spring, he belted clotheslines all over the Fort Lauderdale lot. A close look showed that army life had helped him in one way. He had grown, about 15 pounds worth in the chest and shoulders. He was now 5-11 and a solid 180 pounds. While he could never be considered a Frank Howard or Boog Powell, the days of being the little guy were definitely over.

Manager Houk told the press that Murcer would

be given a try at third base. He'd be competing for the job with veteran Bobby Cox, who played in '69. Cox took one look at Murcer in the batting cage and said, "I don't know if it will be third or not, but that kid will play somewhere this year. I guarantee it."

Cox was right. Murcer opened the season at third base. And just before the opening game, young Bobby told a reporter about his goals for the 1969 season.

"All I want to do is hit .260 this year," he said. "And I want to stick with the club and help out at third base."

So Bobby was being cautious. Then came the opening day in Washington and his long home run, followed by his sensational start and dramatic home run debut at the Stadium. By that time everyone was looking to him as the next Yankee superstar.

There was even some inside pressure on Bobby. In a completely innocent move, Yankee clubhouseman Pete Sheehy gave him Mickey Mantle's old locker, and also uniform number "1," last worn by Bobby Richardson.

"I gave the kid Mickey's locker because I figured it would make him happy," remarked Sheehy. "I know Mickey likes him and they're both from Oklahoma. Someone might as well use it and why not Murcer?"

Still, it served as another reminder to Bobby of just what was expected of him.

None of this bothered him at the beginning of the season. He continued to hit a ton and drive in

baserunners. After two weeks, he ran into a mild slump and went 0-20. This is it, most people thought. The kid will fold now.

But he came out of it April 24, at Cleveland, with a single and two homers. That gave him seven homers in 14 games. He was still hitting .325 and continued to power the ball.

It was the other Yankees who weren't hitting. Both Tresh and Pepitone, expected to take up some of the slack caused by Mantle's retirement, could not get untracked. Neither seemed to want the hat of leadership. Slowly, it was falling on the head of Bobby Murcer.

"Bobby's got the ability and chemistry to make it big," said Yankee president Michael Burke. "I think he has what it takes to be a superstar. You can't say he's a superstar right now, but he's already a star attraction. And he's a star ballplayer."

All the commotion began to make itself felt. Bobby tried to believe the pressure wouldn't get to him, but he couldn't stop it entirely. In early May, he made four errors at third base in two games as the Yanks dropped their 10th contest in 11 decisions.

The following night against the expansionist Seattle Pilots, Bobby slammed a two-run homer in the first, but Seattle bounced back for seven runs in the bottom of the inning. The Yanks couldn't seem to beat anyone.

Then in the third, Pilot's pitcher Martin Pattin decided to take some action against the Yanks' best hit-

ter. He threw in the general direction of Murcer's head. Bobby was furious. On the next pitch he ripped a single to rightcenter. But he didn't stop at first. He kept running and charged right into Seattle shortstop Ray Oyler.

Oyler couldn't let a young kid push him around and the two began wrestling on the ground. By the time both benches emptied, Bobby realized he was at fault and was apologizing. But it was just another indication of the mounting pressure on the young star.

It was soon after that when Houk moved Bobby to rightfield. He knew the youngster was having a terrible time at third and he didn't want it to affect his hitting. "We considered doing this in spring training," Houk said. "So we were prepared to make the move if we deemed it necessary."

Bobby took it well. Shortly after the move to right, he was the big man at the plate again as the Yanks broke out of another slump. On May 13, he made an error in right, but belted a two-run homer. The Yanks lost that night, their sixth straight, then Bobby got them going again.

He had three singles and a pair of RBI's the next night and the team won. Then, two days later, the Yanks went into the ninth losing, 1-0, to California. Bobby came up with two out and runners on second and third. Facing lefthander Rudy May, he ripped a double to right and the Yanks won, 2-1.

On May 17, Bobby doubled to open the fourth inning against the Angels and later scored the first run

of the game as the Bombers won again. And finally, on the 18th of May, Bobby singled behind Jerry Kenney's single, then Joe Pepitone hit one out and the team won again. Four straight wins, and Bobby was in the midst of them all. A more-than-satisfied Ralph Houk said:

"I'll tell you something, this kid could be one helluva ballplayer. Not just a good ballplayer, but a helluva ballplayer."

Bobby was leading the majors in RBI's with 38 and had 10 homers with a .324 batting average after just six weeks. Then came the injured heel and sudden loss of timing. He began slumping, and this time couldn't seem to snap out of it.

Between May 30, and August 4, Bobby hit just two home runs and his batting average fell some 40 points. During a stretch of games earlier in the season, Bobby had driven in 15 runs while all the other Yankees combined had just 16. Now he was having trouble getting anyone across the plate.

"This kind of thing happens to all young hitters," manager Houk said. "They go good for a while, then they begin to fade. When that happens, they start pressing. But Bobby is too good a hitter not to work his way out of it on his own."

But after several weeks, even Bobby was getting down. "Sometimes I don't know what I have to do to get a hit," he said. "Even when I get good wood on one, someone is there to catch it. But I'm not even

hitting the ball that good anymore and I can't understand it. Everything just seemed to go at once.

"At the beginning of the year I hit every ball well and everything was falling in. Now I think I've been robbed of doubles twice in the last four games. Everything seems to be against me."

But in the end, it was really the pressure that was against Bobby. When he was going good, he'd virtually carried the club. As a 23-year-old rookie who was out of competitive baseball for two years, that pace was just too much to ask for over a long season. Furthermore, the hot start just spiked the talk of a new Yankee superstar, and Bobby heard more than his share of predictions. He was also made to feel that it was his obligation, as the chosen one, to continue the Yankee tradition of having a superslugger on the team.

When it was over, the Yanks had repeated their fifth place finish of 1968, but this time played a whisker under .500 at 80-81. And Bobby finished what would have been a very bright rookie season had it not been for the fast start and aura of great expectations that surrounded him.

He appeared in 152 games, collecting 146 hits in 564 trips to the plate for a .259 batting average. After hitting 10 homers in the first six weeks, Bobby's pace slowed, but he still finished with 26 round trippers and drove 82 runs across the plate. It was certainly a fine freshman season, but with the crosstown Mets

winning the pennant, his total performance was all but forgotten by the media and most fans.

Bobby was a popular performer at the Stadium during 1969. He was friendly and courteous to all those with whom he came in contact. He rarely soured, even through the tough months of July and August. But the Yankee rebuilding program was slow. There were no hot prospects in the minor league organization, and other teams in the league were still reluctant to trade with the Bombers. They were all kind of enjoying the mighty Yankees being on the ropes.

The point is this. The Yanks were building a team of singles and doubles hitters. There were no appreciable power men on the horizon. Bobby Murcer was it. Even Tresh and Pepitone had been traded. With his 26 homers and 82 RBI's, he was expected to be the big man, and the pressure on him to take up where Mantle and Company left off was increasing.

Naturally, the men who knew most about the pressure of assuming the role of the big man in the Yankee attack were the two who came before Bobby—Mickey Mantle and Joe DiMaggio.

Someone asked DiMag what kind of pressure there would be on Murcer following the footsteps of himself and Mickey Mantle.

"If he hits .300," Joe D. exclaimed, "there'll be guys who expect him to hit .350. If he hits .350, some people will say he could hit .400.

"Then there will be the boos. Sooner or later they'll

33

boo him. He's just got to learn to accept it. They won't boo him forever. They don't boo anyone forever."

As for Mantle, he left the bite of even more direct comparison, for he and DiMag were both center-fielders.

"If I didn't get to a fly ball, someone would invariably say that Joe would have caught it," Mickey said. "Or if I made a bad throw in a key situation, they'd say DiMag would have cut the runner down. People expected me to do the same things Joe did on the field. When I couldn't do them, the pressure made me try too hard."

For Murcer, the pressure became even greater in 1970 when the Yankees decided he would play in centerfield. "Bobby had the speed and the arm," Houk said. "We knew he was uncomfortable in the infield, although I still believe he would have made it at short or third. He had the tools and he's a plugger. But we wanted him to concentrate on the hitting. We didn't have a centerfielder and we felt it was his best natural position."

Although he knew the comparison with Mantle and DiMaggio would be even more direct, Bobby was happy knowing he had an everyday position. He hoped he could achieve greater consistency than he had the year before.

If Bobby was more consistent in 1970, it certainly wasn't at the high level of proficiency that he had hoped for. In fact, he didn't get his average up above the .250 mark for most of the season. He had to learn

a new position again, but he seemed much more comfortable in center than he had been in the infield.

The problem in 1970 was simple. Bobby couldn't get untracked at the plate. He was having some trouble hitting lefties, was striking out too much, and trying to overpower the ball on too many occasions.

"Bobby still hasn't learned that he's a better hitter when he isn't trying to pull the ball so much," commented Tom Greenwade. "And I think the shift to the outfield set him back a bit. Seems like he always had something to slow him down those first couple of years."

The highlight of the 1970 season came for Bobby on Sunday, June 25. The Yanks were playing a doubleheader at the Stadium against the Cleveland Indians. Bobby was hitless when he came up for the last time in game one. He waited for a fastball and pickled it, sending a sharp liner buzzing into the lower right-field stands for a home run.

Then the first time up in the second game he belted one to almost the exact same spot. Next time up he timed a curve and sent a high, arching drive deep into the seats. It was his third straight homer, and when he came up again, he could feel the tension.

But somehow, he hadn't lost the swing. He picked out a fastball and drove it deep to right. As he dug to first he saw it disappear into the stands for his fourth consecutive homer, tying a major league record of long standing. His teammates congratulated him, but

one long time Yankee fan was heard to yell, "Hey, Murcer, why don't you do that more often?"

That was the problem. Bobby just didn't connect enough in 1970. He finished the year with stats very similar to those of his first season, a .251 batting average, 23 home runs, and 78 runs batted in. It wasn't good enough for the partisans still looking for another Mantle.

Surprisingly enough, the Yanks did better than anyone expected. They were never really in the pennant race because the Baltimore Orioles ran away with the American League's Eastern Division. But they played steady ball and finished second with a 93-69 record. Though Bobby had certainly made a contribution, it was overshadowed by the fine play of others.

Leftfielder Roy White was the club's biggest run producer with a .296 batting average, 22 homers and 94 RBI's. He was developing into a consistent, everyday ballplayer. Rookie catcher Thurmon Munson also contributed with a .302 batting average and 53 RBI's. He was also a fine defensive catcher and handled the pitching staff like a veteran, as well as keeping a check on daring baserunners with his strong arm.

The key to the Yankee success in 1970 was the fine pitching. Lefty Fritz Peterson won 20 games, while righties Mel Stottlemyre and Stan Bahnsen won 15 and 14 respectively. In addition, reliever Lindy McDaniel had an outstanding season, with a 9-5 won-lost record, a 2.01 ERA and numerous saves.

Some thought the team was coming, but one reporter saw it this way.

"The Yankees are still not a second place team," he wrote. "They lack punch at the plate and need some more steady ballplayers. They had a good season because the pitching held up and because they got some breaks. But the team bears no resemblance whatsoever to the Bronx Bombers of old. There is no team leader and no big man with the bat. The play of young Bobby Murcer was again disappointing, and it's beginning to look as if he'll be a solid ballplayer, but nothing more. I look for the team to slip back a few notches next year."

Other baseball people agreed with the prognosis. The Yankees had to do some more building before they'd be bona fide contenders. Yet the team seemed content to go with the same people in 1971. They were satisfied with most of the performances. Of Murcer, there was hope that he could get his batting average up perhaps 25-30 points. He was playing well in centerfield and still doing a good job in the power departments. But there was little talk any more of his becoming another Mantle.

Perhaps it was the lessening of the superstar publicity that took some of the pressure off Bobby. For when he returned to Oklahoma City for the offseason, he began to do some serious thinking about the kind of ballplayer he wanted to be in the future.

Bobby took a long look at himself. He stood 5-11 and weighed a solid 180 pounds. He was a tough

enough individual, but he certainly wasn't a Mantle, Ruth, Gehrig or DiMaggio. "I'm just not going to hit 40 or 50 home runs," he thought to himself. Then he remembered all the times he went up there swinging for the short rightfield fence and found himself topping a slow grounder to second. In addition, the pitchers were getting cute and giving him very little that he could pull.

"I really wasn't satisfied with my first two years in the majors," Bobby said. "Maybe I wasn't another Mantle or DiMaggio, but I was certainly better than I had shown. And it made me mad.

"Before I even went to training camp, I decided that this had to be a new year for me. Since I knew I wasn't going to be a big home run hitter, I figured I'd better start concentrating on average. I decided to work more on my bunting, and try going with the pitch and forgetting the fences. I struck out more than 100 times in each of my first two years, and I wanted to cut down on that, too.

"I guess it took me awhile to get smart. But I felt things would be better for me in 1971. There are certainly many things that a ballplayer can do offensively besides hitting homers. I knew I had to learn to hit with my head as well as my bat."

When the season began, Bobby stayed with his new philosophy. And there was a marked difference in his batting style. He was hanging the liners all over the place, going to center and left as often as he pulled to right. He started out by jumping over the .300 mark

and everyone waited for him to hit his inevitable slump.

But Bobby continued to hit. He was making contact like he did in high school, when you could take a vacation between his strikeouts. There was just one problem. Now that Bobby seemed to be settling into the good groove, the other Yankees were having trouble. Munson was having sophomore jinx problems, Peterson wasn't getting the breaks or the victories, and the bullpen had completely soured. So while Murcer was doing the job, the others weren't and the team was again struggling around the .500 mark.

By midseason, Bobby was still hitting well above .300 and driving in runs. He was chosen the starting centerfielder on the American League all-star team. He responded with one hit in three trips and played a fine game in the outfield. And once again he was being labeled a coming star.

Still, the dull play of the Yanks as a team negated some of Murcer's finer performances. And he began to smart at how his greatest season seemed to be slipping by.

"When the Yanks were always winning and spending each October in the World Series, it was big news whenever someone hit a homer to win a big game. But if I win a game or belt a clutch homer, it doesn't matter because we're still in fourth place."

Yet he certainly wasn't complaining too loudly, "It's sure a lot more fun coming out to the ballpark ev-

ery day than it used to be," he said as an after-thought.

Bobby continued his hot pace. In the second game of a doubleheader at Milwaukee on July 25, he came up to pinch hit late in the game. There were three men on base. With a righthander on the mound, Bobby licked his chops. But he wasn't overanxious. He just wanted to make contact.

The Milwaukee pitcher tried to slip a fast one past Murcer. Around came the quick wrists, followed by the sound that always indicated "good wood." The ball soared toward the right centerfield wall and cleared it with room to spare. It was the first grand slam of his career.

When the 1971 season ended, both Bobby Murcer and the Yankees had done complete turnabouts. The Yanks slipped back to fourth place, managing an 82-80 record, the promise of the season before shattered.

As for Bobby, he finally did what they said he'd do two years earlier. With no prolonged slumps or extended dry spells, he put together a super year. His batting average was .331, just six points behind A.L. champ Tony Oliva. He had collected 175 hits (third best in the League) in 529 at bats. Despite not trying for homers, he still managed to wallop 25 and drive in 94 runs. His walks were up to 91 and he cut his strike outs down to a mere 60.

He was also third in the league in total bases (287), had 25 doubles and six triples. And, as one long-time reporter put it, he "enjoyed the best year of any

Yankee since Mickey Mantle won the Triple Crown in 1956. And that includes playing the finest defensive centerfield since Mantle was a pup."

Naturally, there was superstar talk again. Was Bobby Murcer finally in that category? The most obvious man to ask was Mantle, and he responded quickly.

"If Bobby can put together two or three years like last year, I'd have to say he could be called a superstar," said Mickey. "He certainly doesn't have to hit 50 home runs to do it. I think Bobby is capable of batting .350."

Yank general manager Lee MacPhail agreed. "Bobby's pretty close to being a superstar right now. It just takes a couple of outstanding seasons for him to establish that fact in people's minds."

Manager Houk also had similar thoughts. "If Bobby has another year as good as this one he'll be recognized as a superstar. He's not going to hit 50 home runs. One thing he has to do is take better advantage of his speed. And, of course, if we can get into a World Series, then he'll get national recognition."

The Yanks had the same basic team in 1972. They added a relief pitcher, Sparky Lyle, and he brought the bullpen back singlehandedly, becoming the outstanding reliever in the majors. His presence snapped the team back into pennant contention.

In the meantime, Murcer watchers wondered if their hero would take up where he left off in '71. Bobby quickly gave them his answer.

No!

The 1972 season started like a nightmare. He couldn't hit. Not a lick. It was just like his rookie year. His timing was gone and he couldn't seem to do anything right. When he did hit a solid shot, it was caught. Suddenly, the young Oklahoman was in a make or break situation. The ultimate direction of his career was at stake right here. Would he be an up-and-down player, with good and bad years, streaks and slumps? He had been striving for consistency since coming to the club. He didn't want to let it all slip away now.

But the players' strike had set training back and that might have hurt. By the end of May, Bobby was batting just .206. He had never been that low before. And the team wasn't winning. It was the year Houk promised to get the Yanks back into contention. Now he was hoping panic wouldn't set in.

It was time for someone to take charge. When it happened, the man turned out to be Bobby Murcer. Suddenly, without warning, he began to hit. He slammed out 15 hits in his next 24 at-bats, including two homers and seven RBI's. By mid-June his average was up to .264, and he was driving in key runs with a mixture of homers and doubles, and whatever else it took.

Bobby was again selected for the all-star team (though not as a starter) and his sensational play right before the midseason game produced this comment from Hall of Famer Ted Williams.

"Bobby Murcer is going to be one of the top stars in the league for the next ten years," the Splendid Splinter said. "In fact, he may just be the best player in the league right now. He's a fine hitter already and he's improving in all the other departments. All he needs now is more experience and confidence. Don't forget, he's only 26."

Even the umpires had respect for Bobby. Ron Luciano talked about a game he called behind the plate. "Murcer sees the ball as well as anyone," Luciano said. "He'll tell you exactly where every pitch is. He missed one strike, but then he told me exactly where the ball was and that really impressed me."

By August, Bobby's slugging and Lyle's bullpen work were instrumental in plunging the Yanks in the midst of a four-team fight for the pennant. It came down to the last weeks of the season, when the team finally fell short. Officially, they were fourth with a 79-76 record, but it was closer than that. The club was still lacking that little extra punch that would put it over the top. But no one could fault Murcer.

Bobby had another great season. Despite his slow start, he recovered to hit over .300 during the second half and finished with a respectable .292 average. In the power department he was devastating, with 33 homers and 96 runs batted in, his personal high in both categories. And he was the big man in the clutch, delivering a bevy of key hits all year.

He also collected 314 total bases, 30 doubles, and seven triples. And he scored a career high of 102

runs. There was little doubt that Bobby Murcer had finally arrived.

"Bobby has become a complete player in the last two years," said Ralph Houk. "He has better bat control now and he takes the walk. He'll go to left and leftcenter and he won't give in to the pitchers. We just hope he continues his current pace."

So, in a sense, Bobby Murcer had come full cycle, going from the big buildup, to a big disappointment, and finally to the big success that had always been predicted for him. And he did it his own way, once he realized that he couldn't be the next Mantle or DiMaggio.

It wasn't easy. Perhaps the demise of the Yankees helped. If the club had remained the all-winning dynasty it had been in the past, there might have been more pressure on Bobby to emulate his illustrious predecessors. But with the team in decline for a decade, there was less attention and less of a demand. So Bobby had more freedom to mature in his own way, to become the kind of ballplayer he had to be. There was really no other route to take. He knew he wasn't a superslugger, and if he tried to be one, he'd remain an inconsistent .250 hitter.

Somehow, it's still hard to realize how much pressure was put on Bobby when Ralph Houk made him the Yankee centerfielder. As one sportswriter put it, "Bobby Murcer was thrust into the most glamorous job on baseball's most glamorous team." Perhaps it was the most glamorous job in all of sports. Yet while

it put Bobby under the gun, it also helped him find himself. Looking back at the move, Bobby says:

"Things became easier for me when I moved to the outfield. The infield made me nervous, very nervous. Because of my brief experiences before I entered the service, I was really afraid of making mistakes. Maybe if I went back there now I'd be OK. But when I was playing short and third I was trying to make the club at the same time. So I really had to concentrate. I was tight and my hitting suffered as well. So in that sense they did me a favor when they moved me to the outfield."

Yet the early comparisons, which continued as Bobby's stature grew, eventually became a source of annoyance. As he himself once said after hearing for the umteenth time how he compared with DiMag and the Mick, "When a record gets warped, you throw it away!"

And as another writer so aptly put it, "Bobby stands out in centerfield beside two plaques honoring his predecessors. Yet those plaques haven't gotten a hit in some time now. Let's hear it for what Murcer does as Murcer, not for what he does like or unlike Joe D. and Mickey."

So as Bobby closed the 1972 season and the Yanks ran at a pennant for the first time in eight years, the young star began to get some recognition as his own man. He had shown remarkable consistency and versatility the past two seasons, leading one veteran coach to say, "Bobby Murcer may be the single most valu-

45

able hitter in baseball today, that is, considering his age and his accomplishments."

Well, that may not be entirely true, but Bobby is certainly among the best hitters in baseball. Still playing with a slightly more than mediocre team, Bobby has become an established man with the stick. He hits for average and power, he drives in runs, scores them, keeps his strike outs down, can go to all fields. In addition, he runs the bases aggressively and with brains, and he's become an outstanding center-fielder, though comparisons have hurt him there because his predecessors were exceptional flychasers. Yet, all things considered, Bobby Murcer finally attained his superstar status after the 1972 campaign. He could be denied no longer.

But what about the Yankees? This is the time to take a look at Murcer's team—the ballclub that completely dominated the sport for over 40 years, from the early 1920's until that pennant of 1964.

Perhaps it's best to turn back the clock, to April 18, 1923, when a great event captured the headlines in the sports world. The *New York Times* reported it this way:

"Governors, generals, colonels, politicians and baseball officials gathered together solemnly yesterday to dedicate the biggest stadium in baseball, but it was a ballplayer who did the real dedicating. In the third inning, with two teammates on the base lines, Babe Ruth smashed a savage home run into the right field bleachers, and that was the real baptism of the new

Yankee Stadium. That also won the game for the Yankees, and all the ceremony which had gone before was only a trifling preliminary.

"The greatest crowd that ever saw a baseball game sat and stood in this biggest of all baseball stadia. Inside the grounds, by official count, were 74,200 people . . ."

That, in effect, was the beginning of the Yankee dynasty, though the team had already taken A.L. pennants the previous two seasons. Until 1923, the Yanks shared the older Polo Grounds with the New York Giants. But after '23, the team played at baseball's most modern stadium, and with the coming of Ruth, Gehrig, etc., they had begun building the sport's greatest and most colorful team. To be a New York Yankee in the 20's was the epitome of professional athletic success.

The team was privately owned then, by business tycoons Ed Barrow and Jacob Ruppert. They were also avid sports fans who wouldn't hesitate to part with a dollar when it came to promoting their team or acquiring talent. Thus the Yankee system continued to produce outstanding players to complement the superstars.

So the Yanks became the most successful team in the history of sports, dominating baseball for four decades. The men who managed the team, notably Miller Huggins, Joe McCarthy, and Casey Stengel, became as well known and successful as the players

they directed. The fans continued to flock to the big stadium, and the ballclub never stopped winning.

Even when the ownership passed into the hands of Dan Topping and Del Webb, things remained pretty much the same. DiMaggio was the ranking superstar in the late 30's and 40's, Mantle in the 50's and early 60's. And if there were signs of trouble, of weaknesses in the armor, Topping and Webb were always ready to part with a bundle of cash to get the players necessary to continue winning. Many said it was Yankee money as well as Yankee baseball expertise that kept the Bronx Bombers on top, and that may well be true.

Players shuttled in and out of the Yankee organization in the 50's and early 60's, and the team continued to win. Ralph Houk took over the managerial reigns from Stengel after the 1960 season and promptly won three straight pennants and a pair of World Series. Then, before '64 began, Houk moved into the general manager's chair and turned the field boss job over to longtime star catcher Yogi Berra. And this was the year that marked a turning point in Yankee fortunes for several reasons.

There were problems that season, even though the team seemed to have its usual quantity of good, young ballplayers. There was some trouble between the players and Berra, and the club never got untracked. Perhaps it was difficult for Yogi to suddenly be bossing his teammates of a year earlier. At any rate, it took an 11-game winning streak in mid-Sep-

tember to give the Bombers their fourteenth American League pennant in 16 years.

But that wasn't really the big news. At the outset of the season, the Yanks' new rivals, the crosstown Mets, had opened their new ballpark, Shea Stadium, and had begun drawing huge crowds despite being a tenth-place team. Suddenly, Yankee Stadium seemed old and outmoded, with its limited parking facilities, its many support columns to obstruct the view, and its lack of escalators to the upper tiers. It was a much more pleasant experience to watch a game at Shea.

Then in August there was another shock. Co-owners Topping and Webb announced that they had sold the ballclub for $13.2 million to the Columbia Broadcasting System. The Yankee family was breaking up. Topping and Webb had always operated on a personal level with the players and management. Now, suddenly, the team was owned by a faceless corporation. Everyone wondered what would happen next.

Then came the pennant push and a hard-fought seven-game world series loss to the Cardinals. Shortly afterward, word came that Manager Berra was being fired. Yankee fans seethed. Yogi had been one of the most popular players ever to don pinstripes and everyone blamed C.B.S. for taking a cheap shot at him. When the team began falling apart the next year, there was an I-told-you-so attitude among long-time fans. Yankee attendance continued to drop off, while Mets attendance climbed.

The installation of Michael Burke, a C.B.S. execu-

tive, as Yankee president, and the return of Ralph
Houk as field manager, helped restore the lost
prestige, but it failed to significantly improve the ballclub.

That's about the time Bobby Murcer entered the
picture. "As far back as 1964 I could have signed with
the Dodgers for $11,000 more than the Yanks offered,"
he recalls. "But since the Yankees seemed to be in the
world series every day, I figured I'd make up the difference quickly with a world series check. It didn't
quite work out that way."

No, it didn't. Though Burke was an able adminis-
trator and innovative promoter, and Houk still a dy-
namic field leader, the Yanks couldn't rebound. Perhaps it was the farm system, no longer turning out
enough good ballplayers to stock half the teams in the
league. Perhaps it was those other teams, no longer
willing to ship their prospects and solid vets over to the
Yanks to assure the Bombers additional pennants. Or
perhaps it was a reluctance on the part of C.B.S. to put
out the huge sums of money that Topping and Webb
had always distributed to get what they wanted. At
any rate, it was some combination of those and other
elements. Attendance continued to drop and the team
kept on losing.

The Yankees of 1972 made a run at the pennant,
but many felt it was the inability of any of the other
teams to pull away—rather than the New Yorkers'
talents—that kept them in the race. At any rate,
most experts agreed that you could count the real

quality ballplayers on the Yankees without taking off
your catcher's mitt.

First there was Murcer. Everyone started with him.
Bobby was now acknowledged to be best player on
the team. Then perhaps came Thurm Munson, the
fine catcher. Roy White was a solid outfielder. But after those three, the starting eight were shaky. The
pitching boasted Mel Stottlemyre, perhaps Fritz Peterson, and reliever Sharky Lyle. After that there was
a collection of prospects who hadn't arrived, vets who
never would, and a few older players who had seen
their best years.

With the triumvirate of Burke, Houk, and general
manager Lee MacPhail running the show, the
Yankees took a phrase from George Allen (coach of the
pro football Washington Redskins) and decreed that
the future was now. They began trading some of their
young prospects for seasoned vets in an attempt to
put the Yanks over the top.

One big deal was made with Cleveland, with
young players John Ellis, Charlie Spikes, and Rusty
Torres all leaving New York in favor of Graig Nettles,
a power-hitting third baseman who was expected to
take advantage of the short rightfield porch at the stadium. There was some criticism of the trade, since both
Ellis and Spikes were considered power hitters with a
future. Another deal brought veteran outfielder Matty
Alou to the club. Alou was a proven .300 hitter whom
the Yanks figured would make a perfect number two

or three hitter. Matty would play rightfield, alongside Murcer and Roy White.

So the starting eight looked stronger. The only possible weakness was the keystone combo of Gene Michael at short and Horace Clarke at second. Clarke had definite fielding deficiencies, while Michael didn't hit much and seemed to tire in late season.

The pitching was pretty well set. Stottlemyre, Peterson, Steve Kline, and Mike Kekich were slated to be the starters. Lyle and vet Lindy McDaniel would handle the bullpen. Maybe now the club could make a real run at it. Then things started to happen.

While participating in an off-season golf tournament in Puerto Rico, Bobby Murcer tripped in his motel room and suffered a broken right hand. The Yankee brass shuddered. Losing the big man would really be a blow. But doctors said the break wasn't serious. Bobby would be ready by opening day.

Bobby thought so, too. Three weeks later, with spring training just a few weeks away, Bobby let it be known that he was going to seek a $100,000 salary for 1973. He had made about $75,000 the previous year and was now reaching for the magic number. There had only been two 100-grand players on the Yanks before him. You guessed it: they were DiMaggio and Mantle, and each had taken quite a bit longer to reach that coveted plateau.

When reporters asked Bobby if he was going to take a hard line on negotiations, he left the door open for compromise.

"I won't say that I'm holding to that figure to the penny, but it's definitely what I'm aiming for. I don't think the broken hand will hamper me since doctors are confident it will be as good as ever by opening day."

But there was still another factor involved. In January, 1973, the story broke. After nine years, C.B.S. was selling the Yankees, and the buyers were a large coalition of businessmen, most of them from the Cleveland area and headed by shipbuilder George Steinbrenner III. Steinbrenner's partner was none other than Mike Burke, the Yanks' president, who was leaving C.B.S. to become a part owner of the team. With the flashy Burke continuing to run the show, some thought the Bombers would regain the family feeling of the Topping-Webb era.

One of the first things the new regime did was to grant Bobby Murcer his wish—a $100,000 contract. That not only made Bobby the third Yankee to reach the big figure, but also the youngest player in American League history to achieve that salary level. So Bobby was content and happy, and looking forward to the upcoming season.

"I'll get the final word on the hand by the middle of March," he said. "X-rays show the bone is knitting perfectly. I haven't been able to run much because we've had so much snow in Oklahoma City, but by April 6, I'll be ready."

The transfer of ownership went smoothly, with Burke as the cohesive link, and everyone came to

camp with a positive attitude. Then another bombshell hit. Two Yankee starting pitchers, Fritz Peterson and Mike Kekich, revealed that they had literally traded families during the off-season. Each was living with the other's wife and children and contemplating making the change a permanent one, via divorce and remarriage. It wasn't really that shocking in view of today's social mores, but ballplayers are still folk heroes in the grandest tradition, and the story made headlines all over the country.

The family switch stayed in the news for weeks, as every writer and columnist took pot shots at the two pitchers. The team refused to make a trade and a new form of tension gripped the club. When the season started, both Peterson and Kekich were ineffective, probably a result of the pressure they had placed on themselves. Murcer and Nettles weren't hitting, and the whole thing started to go sour again right from the start.

When there was some hitting, the pitching failed; when there were both, the defense folded or the bullpen sagged. In other words, nothing went right during the first month and a half of the season. The Peterson-Kekich scandal still lingered. The two pitchers weren't speaking and Kekich carped to the press about not being in the team's regular rotation. Finally, the Yanks shipped the disgruntled pitcher to Cleveland, hoping to end at least one problem.

But it seemed that as soon as one was solved, another cropped up. Toward the end of May it was an-

nounced that club president Mike Burke had resigned. Fired was the more accurate word. It seemed as if Burke's flamboyant style, his long hair and turtle-neck look didn't jibe with the new straight-laced owner Steinbrenner. The two also differed on promotional ideas and the general running of the club. So Burke was out. He had been close to the players and totally involved in the everyday running of the club. Many thought this move would deal a fatal blow to any chances the Yanks had.

Then in early June the team made two moves that seemed to turn things around. Coming to New York in cash deals were veteran pitchers Sam McDowell and Pat Dobson, two former 20-game winners. With Kekich gone and Steve Kline suffering from a chronic sore arm, the two vets stepped right into the starting rotation and began winning. So did the Yanks. And leading the resurgence of the Yankee bats was once again Bobby Murcer.

Because of the broken hand, Bobby got a late start in the spring and consequently wasn't in top shape when the season began. But once he started to connect, he looked better than ever. He was becoming more assertive and outspoken, and although he himself denied being the team leader, it was obvious that many of his teammates now looked to him for encouragement. Still, he refused to claim the distinction of being the leader.

"Heck, I'm no leader," he'd often say in his best Oklahoma drawl. "There really isn't a leader on this

club, unless you count Ralph (Manager Houk). Yeah, Ralph Houk's the real leader on this club."

Yet Bobby was taking charge in more ways than one. When the Indians' Gaylord Perry whipped the Bombers early in the year, there was renewed talk about Perry throwing the illegal spitball. The umpires took no action during the game itself, and when the Yanks protested to Commissioner Bowie Kuhn, nothing happened. Then Bobby spoke up, telling reporters that everyone in the league knew what Perry was doing and that Kuhn was "gutless" for not taking direct action. The action earned Bobby a $200 fine from Kuhn, but it further inflamed the Yanks into the fighting spirit of the pennant race.

Despite the incident, Bobby held no animosity toward Perry. The next time the two teams met and Perry was pitching, Bobby caught a fly for the final out of the inning, and before flipping the ball to Perry, made sure it was sopping wet.

"Here, this should save you some trouble," he said, with a grin.

"Much obliged," answered the Indian's ace righty.

So the humor was still there. Sportswriter Dick Schaap has described Bobby as "friendly, cheerful, and outgoing, with a quick wit, an open manner, and a likeable inclination to say whatever pops into his head."

And amidst all of this, the Yanks continued to win. Bobby was leading the way and he had some real help. Third baseman Nettles wasn't hitting for aver-

age, but was driving in runs. Catcher Thurm Munson was over .300 and showing more power than ever before. Young Ron Blomberg, the first baseman, was actually hitting over .400, though Houk played him just against righties, figuring the lefthanded Blomberg couldn't hit lefties. But behind The Boomer was veteran Felipe Alou and you didn't lose much there. Roy White and Matty Alou were also contributing. In effect, it was pretty much a team effort that propelled the Yanks back into the A.L. East race.

The other clubs helped, too. The fact that neither Baltimore, Detroit, Boston, nor the surprising Milwaukee Brewers could pull away kept Yankee hopes alive. A victory on June 9, put the Bombers in first place with a 30-25 mark. It was the first time the team had been out in front since 1964, a long drought by any standards.

Everyone was contributing. Rookie pitcher Doc Medich gave the team another solid starter and designated hitter Jim Ray Hart, acquired from the Giants, was driving in runs at his old pace. Lyle and the veteran Lindy McDaniel were a strong one-two punch out of the bullpen.

By the end of June the Yanks were still leading and people began to take them seriously. The final game that month saw Bobby crack a long, three-run homer to give the club its sixth straight win, the twenty-second in its last 33 games. Several days later, on July 2, *Sports Illustrated* Magazine ran a story on the Yanks. Pictured on the cover were none other than Bobby

and Ron Blomberg, with the caption reading "Pride of the New Yankees." Though Bobby was the team's acknowledged superstar, he still had to share top billing with the youngster Blomberg.

"I'll tell you something," Blomberg told a reporter about that same time. "They made us favorites to win this year and then we went out and dropped our first four games by a combined score of 32-14. It really shocked us. But all along we knew we were better. Now we're finally proving it."

Bobby, too, was feeling pretty good. He looked back on his previous years with the Yanks, then voiced optimism for the future.

"Some of the guys here have gone through pretty tough times together," he said. "But the experience was good and enabled us to learn about one another. The last two years we've had a shot at it but just didn't have enough good players to win.

"But I have a kind of feeling about this team, a feeling that the bad things are all in the past and we can win it ... just like the Yankees are supposed to do."

It was the tradition again, the very thing that had held Bobby back for so long, but this time he was using it to spur his teammates on. He himself was still discouraged about the slow start, even though his average was up to .285.

"I'm hitting so bad that I've broken 12 bats in the last 15 games. That proves I'm not meeting the ball

right. In fact, I even pulled out one of my oldest bats, made in 1965, and I broke it my first time up."

What Bobby didn't realize then was that he was about to go on his best hitting tear of the season, and a hot Bobby Murcer can virtually carry a ballclub.

On July 3, the Yanks won again, boosting their record to 46-34 and taking a four-game lead in the A.L. East. It looked as if they might be ready to blow the race wide open. And around Yankee Stadium everyone was feeling good.

The theme song of the Stadium organist was "Seems Like Old Times," an obvious reference to the Bombers' pennant winning years. Longtime Yank pitching coach Jim Turner put it this way.

"It's just good to walk out there before the game starts and see so many people with notebooks, tape recorders, and cameras. And they're all interested in us again."

Manager Houk was also enjoying the recent successes. It had been so long for him. After another victory, he joked with reporters who asked him to pose with his feet on his desk and big cigar in his mouth.

"Are you kidding," said the Major. "It's been so long since anyone wanted my picture after a game that I can't remember how to pose." Then Houk got serious. "I'd say the entire difference between our team now and the last couple of years is the hitting. It's really fun to just sit back and watch our hitters do the job."

But the smiling wasn't long lived. On the traditional July 4 doubleheader date, the Yanks dropped a

pair of games to the Red Sox, a team that had murdered them all year. Most observers figured the club would bounce back, but Yank publicist Marty Appel later said that was a turning point.

"Somehow, things were never the same after July 4," said Appel. "I can't say exactly what happened, but our definite high point came on July 3, and we never attained that peak again. It wasn't a dramatic slump, but a gradual decline that continued right through to the end of the year."

The club hung on in first place through July, mainly due to the hitting of Bobby Murcer. On July 13, Bobby slammed three consecutive homers off Gene Garber of Kansas City, boosting his output to 18 round trippers in roughly half a season. He was hitting over .300 and was voted the starting centerfielder on the American League all-star team. Most people thought that Murcer would be the A.L. Most Valuable Player if he and the Yanks kept up the pace.

In late July, Murcer appeared on the cover of *Sport* Magazine, this time alone, giving him the distinction of making the covers of the country's two top sports publications within the space of a single month. Only this time the article wasn't a glorification of Murcer's talents. It said that he was the most anonymous $100,-000 ballplayer in the big leagues. Once again, Murcer was compared with DiMag and Mantle and found lacking in the widespread recognition and popularity accorded his two predecessors.

Despite playing in New York, always the best place

for the big-name athlete, Bobby Murcer had never done a commercial or endorsed a product.

"No one's ever asked me," said Bobby. "I always heard how great it was to be in New York, where all the big-money opportunities were, but you'll never prove it by me."

There are undoubtedly several reasons for this. To begin with, the Yanks have been perennial losers since Murcer joined them, and no one likes a loser. And, as the article pointed out, Murcer was more ordinary looking than his predecessors. He didn't have DiMaggio's height or Mantle's muscles, lacked Joe D.'s chiseled features and Mickey's massive neck. Bobby just didn't stand out in a crowd. But in spite of this, he had the easygoing, pleasing personality that could sell products with great credibility.

When sportswriter Dick Schaap contacted a local advertising mogul and big sports buff, and asked him if he ever thought of using Bobby in a commercial, he got this answer:

"Murcer? He's a little guy, isn't he? Invisible. To tell you the truth, his name has never come up. He's got to be the most unheard-of $100,000 ballplayer who ever lived."

If that's not enough to discourage any player, what is? Yet Bobby accepted it and waited for better days. Realistically speaking, he still had the big salary, and the commercial snub was more a matter of pride than money. Nineteen seventy-three could have been the year—until August rolled around.

The Yanks were basically a .500 team during July, yet they managed to hold the lead since no one else got hot. Then on August 3, the bubble burst. A loss dropped the team record to 60-51, and the young Birds of the Baltimore Orioles pulled away from the rest of the pack to take over first.

Suddenly, the Bombers sagged. The pitching became inconsistent. The defense fell apart. Tired ballplayers stopped hitting. As soon as the pennant seemed out of sight it appeared that the team stopped trying. The letdown was too great. One reporter claimed that the only two Yankees who were still scrapping and fighting were Murcer and catcher Munson. The others, the reporter said, seemed to lie down and die.

But while Bobby continued to hit and hustle, and make all the plays, there was one marked difference in his performance. He stopped hitting for power. It's hard to say why. Maybe fatigue. After all, he'd been the club's iron man for three seasons, appearing in almost every game, and the grind of the long season might have been too much. It's to Murcer's credit as a hitter that he kept his average up, since his homer and RBI production fell off sharply. He belted just four circuits from mid-July to the season's end, and that, plus the fact that there weren't as many Yanks on the bases, contributed to the fallout of ribbys.

The team continued to slump. In early September, the club defeated the Milwaukee Brewers, 8-6. The victory wasn't very significant. It was only the Yanks'

twelfth win in 37 games and kept the struggling New Yorkers two games above .500. It also kept them ahead of the Brewers in the battle for fourth place. By now, it was apparent the team would finish no higher.

After the game there was an announcement. The club had traded both Felipe and Matty Alou, to Montreal and St. Louis respectively, indicating that the great experiment of '73 was over and the club was trying to rebuild again. The Yanks were still in trouble. They hadn't regained the old magic, not by a long shot.

What went wrong? It was hard to say. Ralph Houk is one of the most respected managers in baseball. The players love him. He's an eternal optimist and backs his players to the hilt. In other words, he treats them like grown men. Yankee substitute outfielder Ron Swoboda felt that was part of the problem.

"Ralph's philosophy of managing is laissez-faire," Swoboda said. "He leaves everyone alone, basing his theory on the assumption that you get more out of a ballplayer if you don't hassle him. But that only works if you have immense talent and fundamentally sound players. As far as I see it his approach doesn't work, and that's a rotten shame. The situation is a tragedy in itself."

Houk himself was not the same man who posed with feet on desk when times were better earlier in the year. He was down, and that's unusual for him.

"Our defense has hurt our pitching," he said,

slowly. "They play tired, and I don't really know why. But I'm not going to change my ways. When you've been around as long as I have you stay with the things that have worked for you."

But it was obvious that a shakeup was in order. As the season drew to a close it was widely known that the list of "untouchables" wasn't very long. Murcer, Munson, Stottlemyre, Blomberg, Lyle, and a few youngsters. Other than that, everyone else was liable to be traded.

It all ended quietly, the Yanks fourth with an 80-82 record, and everyone disappointed. What made matters worse was that the crosstown Mets had won another divisional title.

As for Bobby, it was another fine year, though disappointing in the power departments in view of his fast start. He played in 160 games, came to bat 616 times, and that's a long season. His 187 hits gave him a .304 average. Among them were 29 doubles, two triples, 22 homers, and 95 RBI's. Bobby walked 51 times and fanned just 67 times. It was another all-star year, solidifying his reputation as one of the league's best all-around players.

But the long year of shock and surprise wasn't over. Immediately after the team's final game, Manager Houk announced that he was resigning, ending a 35-year association with the team. The players were shocked as Houk announced that he personally took the blame for the team's failure to win and felt it was best for everyone if a change was made.

The ball takes funny bounces. Houk's team won just 80 games, finished fourth, and were considered abject failures. In the National League East, the Mets won just 82 games, yet took a divisional title with a strong comeback, making manager Yogi Berra look like a genius.

Yet none of that really mattered. The fact was that Houk was gone and rumors about the real reason he left began seeping out. One was that new owner Steinbrenner had usurped too much authority from the proud Houk and was actually interfering with Houk's everyday running of the club. It was said that Steinbrenner would even send Houk memos directing him to order certain players to get haircuts.

Club morale was at a low ebb. On January 1, 1974, general manager Lee MacPhail resigned to become President of the American League. So the trio of Houk, Burke, and MacPhail had all departed, leaving the players wondering about the new people coming in. Few jobs were secure and the Yankee organization is still in deep trouble as far as producing a winner.

The team is even losing its home for two years, while the Yankee Stadium landmark is completely renovated. A brand new Stadium will rise on the same site, but while the work is being done, the Yanks will be sharing Shea with the Mets.

So the Yankees and Bobby Murcer will be on a strange ballfield in '74. There's no reason to suspect that Bobby won't be the team's big hitter again, but

he may have to alter his style to suit the new ball-park. As Yank publicist Marty Appel said:

"We don't expect Bobby to be as big a power man at Shea as he was at Yankee Stadium. The dimensions are different. Yet he has become a complete ballplayer in every sense of the word and there's no reason to believe he won't be an even bigger star in the two years at Shea and then when the Yanks return to the Stadium."

So Murcer has made it and the Yanks have not. At press time, the Bombers were desperately trying to sign Dick Williams to manage the club in 1974. Williams was the highly successful skipper of the World Champion Oakland A's who walked out on the last two years of a three-year contract with the A's after several disputes with Oakland owner Charles O. Finley. But Finley is working to block the move unless the Yanks offer his club compensation in the form of some players.

The dispute dragged through the trading season and the Bombers only made some minor deals. When Williams, or another man, finally take over the club, there may be some moves, but it's questionable just how significant they can be at this stage. Everyone remembers the Yanks' winning years and no one is exactly willing to give them something for nothing.

It's still not easy for Bobby Murcer to be a Yankee. It took him some five years to get out of the shadow of his illustrious predecessors, and the comparisons still come back to haunt him. But when he was finally

accepted as an outstanding ballplayer in his own right, the team that had been a winner so often in the past couldn't seem to get back on the right track.

"Bobby could have had a pair of MVP prizes already if the team played like it used to," said a longtime Yankee follower. "If he were on a Yankee pennant winner he'd be right up there in the glamour seat, just like Mickey and DiMag. I guess you could say he's a guy in the right place, but at the wrong time."

Statistics show that in 37 seasons, from 1936 through 1972 the centerfielders on the New York Yankees produced 22 .300 seasons, 22 seasons of 25 or more homers, and 13 campaigns of 100 or more RBI's. Six times during that span the centerfielder on the Yanks won the league's Most Valuable Player prize. No other position on any team has produced a record remotely comparable.

Bobby Murcer is carrying on that tradition. He's already added to some of the statistics and has been on the brink of adding to the others. Before he's through, he should make major contributions to all of them.

And, hopefully, before he ends his career, he'll be running out to centerfield for the first game of the world series. After all, that's where Yankee centerfielders are supposed to be.

Bobby Murcer

Statistics

Year	Club	G	AB	R	H	2B	3B	HR	RBI	BA
1964	Johnson City	32	126	34	46	7	4	2	29	.365
1965	Greensboro	126	478	95	154	30	5	16	90	.322
	New York	11	37	2	9	0	1	1	4	.243
1966	Toledo	133	492	69	131	19	9	15	62	.266
	New York	21	69	3	12	1	1	0	5	.174
1967	New York				(In Military Service)					
1968	New York				(In Military Service)					
1969	New York	152	564	82	146	24	4	26	82	.259
1970	New York	159	581	95	146	23	3	23	78	.251
1971	New York	146	529	94	175	25	6	25	94	.331
1972	New York	153	585	102	171	30	7	33	96	.292
1973	New York	160	616	83	187	29	2	22	95	.304
Major League Totals		802	2981	461	846	132	24	130	454	.284